Business Planner
& Bookkeeper
For the Horse Enterprise

by
Sue Ellen Marder, L.L.M.,
Julia M. Flint, M.B.A.,
and Leslie A. Winter, L.L.M.

Breakthrough

For information, address:
Breakthrough Publications, Inc.
Ossining, New York 10562

Cover photograph copyright © Bonnie Kreitler, Kreitler Media Services

Manufactured in the United States of America
5 4 3 2 1 0 9 8   10 9 8 7 6 5 4 3

ISBN: 0–914327–65–8

Contents

1

Creating a Business Plan for Horse Businesses

Dreams and ambitions are important. But what really counts in the business world are results. For any business, a business plan is part of the process for securing financing. However, the business plan is just as important in the success or expansion of an existing business. Studies have found that four out of five businesses that failed in the initial five years did not prepare a business plan. A business plan is the map you use to run a business. It addresses the key issues of management, marketing, financing, expenses, and other aspects of operation that are critical for a successful horse business.

Some of the reasons for horse business failure include:

- Low Volume
- Inadequate Capital
- Improper Location
- Overwhelming Competition
- Ineffective Advertising
- Market Conditions Mis-read
- Poor Management
- Lack of Experience and Know-how

There are probably a dozen or more reasons why businesses fail. Regardless of the reason, one way of helping to guarantee a much higher degree of success when starting a new business, and even continuing with a current ongoing successful business, is to have a business plan.

Horse businesses don't always fall within the parameters of the typical small business. The industry is one with a very high overhead, low profit margins, and an inventory that consumes food, shoes, and medicine. Two of the key reasons for failure listed above, lack of experience and lack of money, are significant problem areas for horse business owners. Development of a comprehensive business plan will reduce the likelihood of failure.

What Is a Business Plan?

The three main functions of a business plan are:

- A basis on which to manage your business.
- A yardstick by which to measure progress and evaluate changes.
- A way to communicate your ideas, research, and plans to others, particularly for financing.

A business plan should be a realistic view of the expectations and long-term objectives for an established or new business. Just as no two businesses are alike, so should no two business plans be alike. Because some issues in a business plan may be more relevant to others, it is important to tailor your plan's contents to suit your individual circumstances. Still, most plans follow the same general structure.

Why Write a Business Plan?

Preparing a satisfactory business plan can be time consuming, but it is an essential exercise. The planning process forces business owners to understand more clearly what their goals are and how and when they can achieve them. Even if no external support (such as financing) is needed, a business plan can play a critical role in helping to avoid mistakes or recognizing hidden opportunities. The underlying objective of preparing a business plan is to insure the success of the business. Here are some of the main reasons why a business plan should be prepared:

1. The business plan provides you with the road map that you need in order to run your business. It allows you to change directions or modify the pace that you set in starting or running a horse business.
2. It will help you determine your cash flow. It can tell you how much money you need, when you will need it, and where it may come from.
3. It helps you to clearly think about what type of horse business you are starting or running, allows you to consider every facet of the business, and raises the questions that you need to answer in order to succeed in your business.
4. It establishes a system of checks and balances for your business so that you can avoid mistakes and sets up benchmarks to keep your business under control.
5. Whether you are starting up a small business or have been running one for some time, it communicates with banks and other investors, showing them that you know where you are, where you are going, and how you are going to get there. This information will help determine the kind of financing you will need.

In addition, the business plan can help you maintain your competitive spirit by making you think through the entire business process. It insures that you analyze your competition, question your methods, and review your history. A yearly review of your business plan gives you a clear picture of where you are spending your money and where you can increase or reduce spending. It can even regenerate your passion for your horse business!

How Planning Is Critical

- Planning gives you a path to follow. It makes your future what you want it to be.
- It is the most important guide to starting, building, and managing a successful business.
- It is the best tool available to help a small business raise money.
- A business plan can be a communications tool for investors, suppliers, employees, and others interested in the operations and goals of your business.
- If you don't plan for the success of your business, you will fail. It is that simple!

Planning is the most important part of starting and running a successful business. Unless you know where you are going, you will end up somewhere else!

The information that goes into a business plan comes from various sources. If you have an existing business (and, for some reason, have not yet completed your business plan!), you can create the financial part of the plan based on historical figures from your sales and expenses. If you are planning to start a new business, the financial information must come from research and projections. Because of the cyclical nature of a typical horse business, sales and expense projections can vary widely. Take into account that there will be slow months (the winter, for example, for a riding stable) and extremely busy months (the summer months for a riding program in a seasonal resort area).

If you are just starting a business, the financial portion of your plan should include:

- Projected "start-up costs."
- Expected profit for the first year.
- Projected income statement and balance sheet for three years.
- Projected monthly cash flow statement for 12 months, expanded quarterly for a three-year projection.

If you have a young or established business, your plan should include:

- Income statement and balance sheet for the last two years.
- Projected income statement and balance sheet for the next three years.
- Projected monthly cash flow statement for 12 months, expanded quarterly for a three-year projection.

If you have an existing business, the descriptive part of your business plan should be based on your past objectives, products and services you have been successful with, and the current management and organization.

For a new business, detail how you feel your business will function best—what products and services do you think your customers will require most? Explain how you plan to market these products and services. The number of employees and their skill level is an important factor.

The business description should identify your business name, address and owner information, your goals and objectives, and why you are or why you want to be in business. Include a very descriptive explanation of all products and services, describing what you are selling and why. Because sales and marketing are the core of your business, your plan should address several basic questions: Who and how large is your market? How will you be competitive? What pricing and sales terms are you planning? How will you market your products and services?

Your business plan should summarize your goals and objectives and send a message that you are committed to the success of your business. It should be complete, clear, neat and accurate; it will be an extension of you and your business. The length of a good plan will vary from a few pages to well over a hundred pages. The plan should provide a sound "blueprint" for your business and entice any reader to want to know more.

The obstacles to running a thriving horse business are very real. However, they must be overcome if you are to be successful. While we may find it difficult to face the future, heading into it without any direction is much worse. A business plan provides you with a map to lead you to your goal—a profitable and growing business!

What Are the Elements of the Business Plan?

The seven basic sections of a business plan are:

A. Executive Summary: A summary of the basic business idea. (2-3 pages)
B. Description of the Business: Concept and purpose. (1-2)
C. Objectives: Five-year goals. (1-2)
D. Management and Organization (1-2)
E. Products and Services: What you are selling. (1-2)
F. Market Analysis: Who will buy the product or service. (2-3)
G. Marketing Strategy: How the product/service will be sold. (2-3)
H. Financial Projections: Cash required for expenses. (2-3)

A. Executive Summary

The Executive Summary is a critical portion of an effective business plan. It explains your business concepts and practices and lets potential investors know your purpose for being in business. The Executive Summary can be written last (and should be presented first). By writing the Executive Summary after you have written all of the other sections of the plan, you can develop a comprehensive section that concisely describes your business.

Begin the Executive Summary by explaining when your company was formed and what you will be selling. Then explain your business purpose: Describe what products or services you will provide and why your customers will buy them. Explain the phase of operation your business is in; for a new business, describe your start-up activity. If you have an existing business, indicate where you will cut operating costs and how you will increase sales or service income. Give background information on your market and your customers' buying habits, how you will market your product or service, and what type of products or services you sell. If you have an existing business, show how much your business has produced in annual sales or service over the past two years. Give financial projections for the next fiscal year, and include the percentages for your annual growth rate for the next five years.

Explain the concept for your product or service—you might compare other products or services that you know of. Describe any special training that you or your staff will need to maintain your business. Illustrate the marketing strategies you plan to use to meet the competition, as well as the market share you plan to gain. Define your target market by describing a typical customer, and indicate any additional products or services you believe this market might respond to. Have you talked to potential customers? Was their response favorable?

The Executive Summary is also referred to as the "Statement of Purpose." If a potential investor or lender were to read only the Executive Summary, they would know all of the basic details of your business. If your business plan is not to be used for investment or loan purposes, the Executive Summary provides you with a summary of your business and its objectives.

B. Description of the Business

This portion of the business plan will provide a picture of the industry, a profile of your business, and a description of your specific market. It should include the industry background—how big, how many different segments, and what the trends have been. What is the growth potential based on these trends? Are there any new products or services that will make your business more attractive to potential customers? What is the economic outlook for the industry? Are current spending trends favorable for horse businesses?

Next, you should describe the nature of your business. What are the local factors that influence your success? Describe economic factors, cyclical trends, whether you depend on specific vendors or suppliers, and the physical space, inventory, and equipment required for your business. Discuss the staff and training needed, and detail the necessary credentials that you, personally, have for running this business.

Finally, define your target market by structuring a market profile. State who your customers are, the geographical scope of your market, the growth potential, your ability to meet your market's demands, and the demographics of a single customer (age, income, sex, occupation, etc.).

C. Objectives

This key element of the business plan explains the objectives of the business in terms of the results you want to achieve in either the long or short range. Aside from the obvious objective of making a profit, your goals should relate to your expectations as a horse business owner and reflect the underlying reasons for running your business. What are the central purposes and activities of the business? What are its major objectives and strategies? Try to list four measurable objectives that will drive the business. What is your main mission? What do you foresee accomplishing in the future?

D. Management and Organization

This section is an explanation of how the business will be run and how the work will be done. Introduce the management team, whether it be yourself or a set of partners.

5

Indicate whether you will have employees and whether they will be full-time or part-time. Detail what types of tasks you expect them to accomplish (no need to put in full job descriptions, however). Discuss the structure of the company—if official titles are used, who is usually in charge of day-to-day stable operations, stable care, ordering supplies, etc.

If just *one* person is responsible for all of those tasks, indicate that as well. Explain how you'll accomplish this work—list outside services if you'll hire others to help with showing horses, vanning, or other tasks. Describe how you'll handle overloads or down-time and whether you'll hire temporary help. This section can be in list format: List out each person, what his/her title is (if applicable), and specifically what his/her responsibilities are.

E. Products and Services

This section describes your basic products and services. Explain what makes your products and services special. List exactly what you are providing or selling—you may want to use an outline approach, particularly if you are planning to promote several retail items in conjunction with a particular service. Describe each product or service stating what each of them offers. Try and keep the descriptions brief, but be thorough.

F. Market Analysis

This element of the business plan is one of your most critical. It requires some research, a thorough knowledge of the industry (both local and regional), and a description of the known customers for your services or products. Your market analysis should describe the type of customer you will be targeting, including demographic information (age, sex, income level, athletic ability, where they live/work, etc.). Look at market trends and industry competition, including strengths and weaknesses of your competitors, both direct (businesses operating exactly like yours, offering the same product or service to the same market) and indirect (businesses selling products or services related, but not identical, to yours). Find out why they are popular or why customers do not return to them. State how you will be able to best serve the market with your products and services.

G. Marketing Strategy

This section of the business plan outlines a marketing strategy and includes the information behind the decisions. List all of the methods you plan to use for advertising (Yellow Pages, direct mail, trade publications, customer referrals, shows, etc.) and describe them briefly. Explain the benefits of each method, how they will be used and how often, how the strategy will be administered (including measurements to verify that it's working), and the percentage of sales you plan to allocate to marketing. Discuss again your competition and how you will make your services or products unique. Describe your methods for publicity and merchandising. Discuss your market research techniques.

H. Financial Projections

Your financial projections will be fully detailed in the appendices, which should include simple tables of information for your projected income statement, balance sheet, and cash flow. From these tables, make a comprehensive overview and interpret the information in a summarized form. Describe your start-up costs (if applicable) or show the details of capitalization. Show how much money will be needed to bring your product or service to market. Indicate the funds that will be necessary to maintain the business until it becomes profitable. Include descriptions of equipment that will be depreciated and horses that will be purchased. Forecasts should be developed for a three- to five-year period.

Your income statement depicts the total profit or loss of your company by showing the net difference between total revenues and total costs. Income statement information should be presented on a monthly basis for the first three years; total annual amounts are adequate for the remaining projected years.

Your balance sheet shows the worth of your company's assets—cash, accounts receivable, inventory, equipment, land, etc.—and also shows the company's liabilities—accounts/notes payable, taxes payable, interest payable, salaries payable, etc. Balance sheet information should be presented on a quarterly basis for the first three years; thereafter, an annual balance sheet is adequate for projections.

Your cash flow statement will demonstrate the expected revenues and expenses over a period of time. The cash flow totals are the best picture of changes occurring in your business and market. When you estimate cash flow, be conservative, but remember to be realistic. Cash flow information should be presented on a quarterly basis for the first three years; thereafter, annual cash flow projection totals are adequate.

Follow-Up

Once you have created your business plan, don't file it under "never have to look at this again"! In fact, you should update your business plan supporting documents on a quarterly basis as you are able to put in actual (versus planned) figures. Your business plan will then serve as a gauge for your business—how you are doing, how close your estimates were, and what changes are needed for the next quarter to meet your expected revenue goals.

The information from your current bookkeeping system can be tied into your financial projection worksheets. Enter the current actual numbers as you get them and compare them to your estimated numbers. Make the necessary adjustments to future estimated numbers to help determine where to increase or decrease spending in order to reach your sales objectives.

Other Information

There are various software programs on the market that can assist you with developing a business plan. Some of them are "shareware," available from online services, that require only a nominal fee to the author to use them. Others are off-the-shelf packages that can be purchased at your local computer or office supply store. While these packages can be a tremendous help with the automation of your financial statements, it is recommended that you do your own research and generate your own business and marketing text for your business plan. Many of today's spreadsheet programs offer business plan "templates" that can be used in developing your financial statement projections.

Other information on developing a business plan can be found by contacting the Small Business Administration at 1-800-8-ASK-SBA. You may also look to State Economic Development Agencies, Chambers of Commerce, local colleges, and your local library for information.

2

Business Plan Questionnaire & Worksheets

Use this questionnaire to fill in some of the important elements necessary for your business plan.

Cover Page

Business Name: _____

Address: _____

_____

Telephone: _____

Contact Person: _____

A. Executive Summary (write this section *last*, after completing all other sections)

1. What is your ultimate goal (your "mission") for this business: _____

_____

_____

_____

_____

2. What makes your product/service unique: _____

_____

_____

_____

_____

3. What are your projections (sales, expenses, profits): _____

_____

_____

_____

_____

4. What are your financial needs (if applicable): _____

_____

_____

_____

B. Description of the Business

1. Describe the industry: _____

_____

_____

_____

_____

2. Describe the growth potential for your business: _____

_____

_____

_____

3. Describe any new products or developments related to your business: _____

_____

_____

_____

_____

4. Describe any economic trends that are favorable to your business: _____

_____

_____

_____

_____

5. Describe the overall outlook for your industry: _____

_____

_____

_____

_____

6. What is the exact description of your business: _____

_____

_____

_____

_____

7. List any plans for research and development for your business: _____

_____

_____

_____

_____

C. Objectives

1. What are your long-term goals (size of business, geographic range, etc.): _____

_____

_____

_____

_____

2. Do you want to make this a family business and, if so, who would be involved: _____

_____

_____

_____

_____

3. How do you plan on developing your list of suppliers: _____

_____

_____

_____

_____

4. What profits do you expect to make (list for years one through five): _____

_____

_____

_____

_____

5. Do you have any current debt and, if so, how do you expect to pay that down: _____

_____

_____

_____

_____

D. Management and Organization

1. Who started the business: _____

_____

_____

_____

_____

2. Who will be running the day-to-day operations of the business:

_____

_____

_____

_____

3. List the members of the management team:

_____

_____

_____

_____

4. List the functions of the management team:

_____

_____

_____

_____

5. List the responsibilities of all other staff:

_____

_____

_____

_____

6. List any outside support you may use (attorneys, accountants, blacksmiths, temporary help, veterinarians, etc.):

_____

_____

_____

_____

7. Describe how you plan to compensate your management, staff, and outside support:

_____

_____

_____

_____

_____

_____

_____

E. Products and Services

1. List your products and services: _____

_____

_____

_____

_____

_____

_____

2. Describe, for the products and services listed above, your customers' benefits from using

these products and services: _____

_____

_____

_____

_____

_____

_____

3. Identify the seasonal cycle for your services (busy and slow seasons): _____

_____

_____

_____

_____

_____

F. Market Analysis

1. Describe your market: _____

_____

_____

_____

_____

_____

2. Estimate your market share for years one through five: _____

_____

_____

_____

_____

3. Estimate the market stability and market growth for years one through five: _____

_____

_____

_____

_____

4. Customer Profile:

    Age: _____

    Income: _____

    Sex: _____

    Occupation: _____

    Family size: _____

    Culture: _____

    Education: _____

    Geographical location: _____

    Years in area: _____

    Experience with horses: _____

    Attitude toward horses: _____

    Other: _____

    _____

    _____

5. List your competitors: _____

    _____

    _____

    _____

    _____

    _____

6. Describe how your competitors are promoting their products and services: _____

    _____

    _____

    _____

    _____

    _____

G. Marketing Strategy

1. Will you have sales personnel? If so, what will be their qualifications: _____

_____

_____

_____

_____

2. List your planned advertising and promotion methods: _____

_____

_____

_____

_____

3. Describe your techniques of monitoring your marketing strategy: _____

_____

_____

_____

_____

H. Financial Projections

Income Statement Information

1. Projected revenues:

Year One

Jan	Feb	Mar	Apr	May	June	July	Aug	Sept	Oct	Nov	Dec

Year Two

Jan	Feb	Mar	Apr	May	June	July	Aug	Sept	Oct	Nov	Dec

Year Three: total annual revenues: _____

Year Four: total annual revenues: _____

Year Five: total annual revenues: _____

2. Cost of goods/services sold, *supplies*:

Year One

Jan	Feb	Mar	Apr	May	June	July	Aug	Sept	Oct	Nov	Dec

Year Two

Jan	Feb	Mar	Apr	May	June	July	Aug	Sept	Oct	Nov	Dec

Year Three: total annual COGS/supplies: _____
Year Four: total annual COGS/supplies: _____
Year Five: total annual COGS/supplies: _____

3. Cost of goods/services sold, *labor*:

Year One

Jan	Feb	Mar	Apr	May	June	July	Aug	Sept	Oct	Nov	Dec

Year Two

Jan	Feb	Mar	Apr	May	June	July	Aug	Sept	Oct	Nov	Dec

Year Three: total annual COGS/labor: _____
Year Four: total annual COGS/labor: _____
Year Five: total annual COGS/labor: _____

4. Selling: Commissions

Year One

Jan	Feb	Mar	Apr	May	June	July	Aug	Sept	Oct	Nov	Dec

Year Two

Jan	Feb	Mar	Apr	May	June	July	Aug	Sept	Oct	Nov	Dec

Year Three: total annual selling/commissions: _____
Year Four: total annual selling/commissions: _____
Year Five: total annual selling/commissions: _____

5. Selling: Advertising

Year One

Jan	Feb	Mar	Apr	May	June	July	Aug	Sept	Oct	Nov	Dec

Year Two

Jan	Feb	Mar	Apr	May	June	July	Aug	Sept	Oct	Nov	Dec

Year Three: total annual advertising: _____
Year Four: total annual advertising: _____
Year Five: total annual advertising: _____

6. General/Administrative

Year One

	Jan	Feb	Mar	Apr	May	June	July	Aug	Sept	Oct	Nov	Dec
Salaries												
Payroll Taxes/Benefits												
Vehicle Expense												
Insurance												
Professional Services												
General Business Expense												
Stable Supplies												
Postage												
Office Supplies												
Telephone												
Rent												
Utilities												
Depreciation												
Travel & Entertainment												
Miscellaneous												

Year Two

	Jan	Feb	Mar	Apr	May	June	July	Aug	Sept	Oct	Nov	Dec
Salaries												
Payroll Taxes/Benefits												
Vehicle Expense												
Insurance												
Professional Services												
General Business Expense												
Stable Supplies												
Postage												
Office Supplies												
Telephone												
Rent												
Utilities												
Depreciation												
Travel & Entertainment												
Miscellaneous												

Year Three: total annual G&A: _____

Year Four: total annual G&A: _____

Year Five: total annual G&A: _____

Balance Sheet Information

1. Current Assets

Year One:

Mar	June	Sept	Dec

Year Two:

Mar	June	Sept	Dec

Year Three: total annual Current Assets: _____

Year Four: total annual Current Assets: _____

Year Five: total annual Current Assets: _____

2. Cash

Year One:

Mar	June	Sept	Dec

Year Two:

Mar	June	Sept	Dec

Year Three: total annual Cash: _____

Year Four: total annual Cash: _____

Year Five: total annual Cash: _____

3. Accounts Receivable

Year One:

Mar	June	Sept	Dec

Year Two:

Mar	June	Sept	Dec

Year Three: total annual Accounts Receivable: _____

Year Four: total annual Accounts Receivable: _____

Year Five: total annual Accounts Receivable: _____

4. Inventory

Year One:

Mar	June	Sept	Dec

Year Two:

Mar	June	Sept	Dec

Year Three: total annual Inventory: _____
Year Four: total annual Inventory: _____
Year Five: total annual Inventory: _____

5. Fixed Assets

Year One:

Mar	June	Sept	Dec

Year Two:

Mar	June	Sept	Dec

Year Three: total annual Fixed Assets: _____
Year Four: total annual Fixed Assets: _____
Year Five: total annual Fixed Assets: _____

6. Equipment

Year One:

Mar	June	Sept	Dec

Year Two:

Mar	June	Sept	Dec

Year Three: total annual Equipment: _____
Year Four: total annual Equipment: _____
Year Five: total annual Equipment: _____

7. Accumulated Depreciation

Year One:

Mar	June	Sept	Dec

Year Two:

Mar	June	Sept	Dec

Year Three: total annual Accumulated Depreciation: _____
Year Four: total annual Accumulated Depreciation: _____
Year Five: total annual Accumulated Depreciation: _____

8. Accounts Payable

Year One:

Mar	June	Sept	Dec

Year Two:

Mar	June	Sept	Dec

Year Three: total annual Accounts Payable: _____
Year Four: total annual Accounts Payable: _____
Year Five: total annual Accounts Payable: _____

9. Payroll Taxes Payable

Year One:

Mar	June	Sept	Dec

Year Two:

Mar	June	Sept	Dec

Year Three: total annual Payroll Taxes Payable:_____
Year Four: total annual Payroll Taxes Payable:_____
Year Five: total annual Payroll Taxes Payable:_____

10. Long-Term Liabilities: Notes Payable

Year One:

Mar	June	Sept	Dec

Year Two:

Mar	June	Sept	Dec

Year Three: total annual Notes Payable: _____
Year Four: total annual Notes Payable: _____
Year Five: total annual Notes Payable: _____

11. Prior Year Profit or (Loss)

Year One:

Mar	June	Sept	Dec

Year Two:

Mar	June	Sept	Dec

Year Three: total annual Prior Year Profit or (Loss): _____
Year Four: total annual Prior Year Profit or (Loss): _____
Year Five: total annual Prior Year Profit or (Loss): _____

12. Current Year Profit or (Loss)

Year One:

Mar	June	Sept	Dec

Year Two:

Mar	June	Sept	Dec

Year Three: total annual Current Year Profit or (Loss): _____
Year Four: total annual Current Year Profit or (Loss): _____
Year Five: total annual Current Year Profit or (Loss): _____

13. Common Stock

Year One:

Mar	June	Sept	Dec

Year Two:

Mar	June	Sept	Dec

Year Three: total annual Common Stock: _____
Year Four: total annual Common Stock: _____
Year Five: total annual Common Stock: _____

Cash Flow Projections

Use the Cash Flow Projection worksheet to determine your cash flow for each month for the first three years. Take quarterly totals for each of the line items and insert those totals into the Quarterly Cash Flow Projection worksheet. Then, list annual totals for years three, four, and five here:

Year Three: total annual Cash Flow Projection: _____

Year Four: total annual Cash Flow Projection: _____

Year Five: total annual Cash Flow Projection: _____

3

Sample Business Plan for a Small Horse Business

Horses 'R' Us
123 Main Street
Small Town, USA 10000
123/345-4567

John S. Smith

January 1, 1996

TABLE OF CONTENTS

EXECUTIVE SUMMARY

Horses 'R' Us was formed as a proprietorship in December, 1995, in Small Town, USA, by John S. Smith in response to the following market conditions:

- Start-up opportunities exist in the horseback riding industry.
- I have several customers who are willing to sign up for long-term riding instruction within the next three months.
- Several other prospective customers have expressed serious interest in boarding their horses with Horses 'R' Us within six months.

I previously worked at a company that was active in the horse industry. Over the past few years I spent much time studying ways to improve overall service and increase profits. This plan is a result of that study.

The basic components of this plan are:

Horseback Riding Instruction

- Competitive pricing
- Expand the markets
- Increased advertising
- Lower our overhead costs
- Thereby achieving higher profits

Horse Boarding

- Sign contracts
- Increased advertising
- Increase staff

Financial Goals

	Year 1	Year 2	Year 3
Sales (000's)	650.00	3,880	16,649
Net Income	99.03	1,120.83	16,649

30

THE MANAGEMENT

President   John S. Smith

<u>Qualifications</u>

Employed at: Mary Doe Co. 1990-1995
                      Horse boarding and instruction

Education: University of Connecticut
                      Storrs, CT
                      B.S. - Management

<u>Short Biographies</u>

President
John S. Smith was previously employed as the boarding manager at Mary Doe Co., a well-known horse boarding and riding instruction business. Mr. Smith graduated from the University of Connecticut in 1985 with a bachelor's degree in management. Mr. Doe will be employed by the Company on a full-time basis.

Bookkeeper/Office Manager
Alice Wade was formerly employed as bookkeeper for ABC Horse Stables, a position she held for 10 years prior to joining Horses 'R' Us. Ms. Wade graduated from Metropolitan City College in Mobile, Alabama, in 1976 with a bachelor's degree in accounting. Ms. Wade will be employed by the Company on a full-time basis.

Boarding Manager
Joe Stokes supervises the overall operations of the horse stables. He was formerly employed by RQW Company as the training instructor. He brings with him an extensive knowledge of horses and an associates degree in business from Charter Community College in Albany, New York. Mr. Stokes will be employed by the Company on a full-time basis.

Responsibilities
John S. Smith, President - Responsible for entire operation. Oversees management function and all other staff. Salary - $60,000.

Alice Wade, Bookkeeper/Office Manager - Responsible for financial operations, accounts payable, accounts receivable, interaction with suppliers, customer service. Salary - $40,000.

Joe Stokes, Boarding Manager - Responsible primarily for overall operations of the horse stables. Salary - $35,000.

HORSES 'R' US HISTORY

In December, 1996, I formed a horse product and service company that provided horse riding instruction and boarding services to the family-oriented, athletic market. This company was located in Small Town, USA. I formed this company as a proprietorship.

The main goal of this company was to provide affordable riding instruction for those members of the community who wished to ride horses but could not care for one on their own and to board horses for those members who owned their own horses but could not care for one at their own site.

Financing was arranged through friends and family as gifts and investments.

This venture was very successful in generating and increasing sales, but was not effective in achieving profitability. The main reason for this was the amount of actual overhead experienced, which was not initially anticipated by me at the beginning of that venture. Items including shortage of hay resulting in higher prices, cost of additional school horses, and extraordinary veterinarian bills were expenses not originally forecast or expected. With this level of overhead, it was mathematically impossible to achieve profitability.

OR:

This business was very successful in generating and increasing sales, as well as effective in achieving profitability. This was due to the following reasons:

- No other horse businesses existed in the area.
- We provided the community with a new form of exercise.
- Our stable manager took great pains to make sure that the animals were well taken care of, resulting in new boarders.

OR:

Horses 'R' Us was recently conceived and is still in the beginning stages. To this point the following has been accomplished:

- The following team has been formed: John S. Smith, President, responsible for the entire operation; Alice Wade, Bookkeeper/Office Manager; and Joe Stokes, Boarding Manager.
- A prospective customer list has been compiled.
- Strategy meetings are being held every Friday evening.
- This business plan has been drawn up.

We are now able to adequately address the markets we have targeted. We have adjusted our staff, redirected our advertising, and have added the sales prospects (show jumpers) and services necessary to meet the needs and expectations of our customers.

PRODUCT AND SERVICE DESCRIPTION

Horses 'R' Us intends to offer horseback riding instruction and horse boarding, as well as the associated products necessary to ride and board horses. We offer:

Horseback Riding Products

- Offers the lowest price on the market
- Offers the most technically advanced
- Offers more useful features
- Saves time and money
- Offers better value per dollar spent
- Products are delivered to our warehouse on a timely basis and stored properly

Horseback Riding Instruction Service

- Provides a service that is not currently available in this area
- Is strengthened by a team with combined experience of 35 years
- Trainers are experienced in show jumping and dressage
- Instruction in jumping, dressage, and fox hunting
- Students participate in classes consisting of same-age and ability groups
- Saves money
- Provides an alternative, cost-effective way to exercise

Horse Boarding Service

- Provides a service that is not currently available in this area
- Is strengthened by a team with combined experience of 35 years
- Boarders are mature, experienced riders
- Stable manager addresses specialized areas such as grooming, feeding, and exercise
- Arrangements are made for the special care of young horses in training and horses with chronic injury problems
- Saves money
- Provides a cost-effective way to board horses

Even though at this time our expertise is unique in the marketplace, we expect advances to be made and competitors to arise and offer similar services. We will meet this challenge by:

- Hiring staff specialized in these areas
- Increasing our continuing education and training expense
- Adding additional services for the busy amateur riders
- Making regular investments in new equipment

OBJECTIVES

Long Term

Horses 'R' Us believes very strongly in technical, financial, business, and moral excellence. To secure a stable future for all those connected with Horses 'R' Us, we have set the following long term goals:

- Present market is estimated at $XXX. Our goal for market share is XX%.

- We want to be considered by our peers to be the market leader in sales and service as evidenced by:

  - Year-end awards from A.H.S.A. or affiliates
  - High end of scale in horse sales
  - Major market share of boarding in this area
  - Technical excellence of professional staff
  - Community involvement (organization of horse shows for local charities)

Short Term

- Market share goals

  First Year   XX%
  Second Year   XX%
  Third Year   XX%
  Fourth Year   XX%

- Decrease or maintain costs through acquisition of new equipment.

- Increase productivity by investing in employee training and education.

  1. Budget for complete computer training for appropriate applications.
  2. Set up and maintain employee training program.
  3. Budget for necessary clinics and/or continuing job-specific education.

- Maintain state-of-the-art accounting system for careful tracking.

- Monthly reports on financial status versus the industry.

- Aggressive recruitment of the best staff in the industry.

- Support company involvement in various local and national charity events.

OUR COMPETITIVE ADVANTAGES

The distinctive competitive advantages that Horses 'R' Us brings to this market are:

- *Experience* in this market. We have 35 years of hands-on experience in this industry.

- *Sophistication* in finance and management. This results in our being the low-cost supplier in these price sensitive markets.

  - The philosophy of Horses 'R' Us is to price not just according to our costs, but also according to what the market will pay.

    - Our targeted minimum gross profit margin for a category must be XX%.

    - By pricing to the market, higher sales will be achieved and therefore increase buying power.

    - The stable will include a range of financing arrangements as well as early payment discounts.

  - Rather than being strictly local, we will expand into the regional market.

- *Capitalization* policies that will allow us to fully address the respective markets with comprehensive marketing and customer service plans.

  - By keeping overhead low, profits can be funneled back into operations thus avoiding high debt ratios or lost sales opportunities.

  - A quarterly direct mail campaign will be directed at both current customers and prospective new customers consisting of an informative newsletter called, "What's New Is Horses 'R' Us."

  - A toll-free national 800 number will be used for customer orders and inquiries.

  - A complete four-color catalog will be printed on a yearly basis. Price lists will be updated as needed. Aggressive advertising in trade magazines will be planned.

  - Consideration will also be given to attending horse shows around the area.

- With this level of capitalization, should an unexpected downturn occur, we will be able to continue operations on a positive scale.

- *Innovation.* We have a history of innovative ideas.

Horseback Riding and Horse Boarding Products

Through my leadership, we will be able to reduce overhead as a percentage of sales thereby increasing the amount of profit to be retained in the business. Because of our pricing policy, more people will purchase our merchandise thus increasing the size of the market, and we will increase our market share. What Horses 'R' Us proposes to use is just good solid business sense, economies of scale, and the use of efficient financial techniques. This will allow us the following options:

- increase service
- increase advertising
- reduce prices
- increase profits
- increase selection

Horseback Riding Instruction and Horse Boarding Services

Through my leadership, we will be able to reduce overhead as a percentage of sales thereby increasing the amount of profit to be retained in the business. What Horses 'R' Us proposes to use is just good solid business sense, economies of scale, and the use of efficient financial techniques. This will allow us the following options:

- increase customer service by offering more levels of instruction at convenient times
- increase advertising expenditures
- increase profits
- increase selection of boarding services offered

This plan will give us tremendous flexibility to use any of these options or a mix of them to effectively attack our target markets and meet our long term goals. This combination of experience, sophistication, capitalization, and innovation will assist Horses 'R' Us as it strives to reach its sales, profit, and return objectives.

PRICING

Horseback Riding and Horse Boarding Products

Before we set the price for these products, we determined on a unit basis what the costs were going to be. We then determined what the market price was for the normal widget. At this price it was determined that for all but the lowest sales projections these products would turn a profit at this price. However, since our products offer additional features, we felt that we could price it approximately 50% above other inferior products.

To test this price, we polled 50 large users of these products. We first questioned them about the desirability of our extra features and then asked them directly if this price would be acceptable if such a product were available. We found that 75% of those polled would be interested in these products. Of this 75%, we received 10 firm orders representing approximately 30% of this group.

OR:

We have determined that the market price is $ XX per unit. This will equal a margin of XX%.

OR:

Our unit cost has been figured at $XX. We need a margin of XX% to pay our overhead and earn a sufficient profit. Therefore, our selling price will be $XX.

Horseback Riding and Horse Boarding Services

Before we set the price for our services, we forecast what our fixed monthly costs were going to be. We then determined the market rate for comparable lessons and boarding facilities. At this rate it was determined that for all but the lowest billing projections, these services would turn a profit.

SPECIFIC MARKETS

Market #1

General History

Horse businesses have enjoyed a period of steady growth over the past 20 years. This demand is due to many factors, not the least of which is the advance of horse care technology. In our proposed marketing area, there are no horse care services.

Entry Strategy

Over the past few years, we have noticed an increase in demand for full horse care services—not just boarding and riding. Our computerized office allows us to track our customer needs and schedule instruction or extra care on one hour's notice.

We intend to attack this market very aggressively through the use of:

1. Advertisements in local periodicals.
2. Radio advertisements on weekends.
3. Yellow pages advertisements.

As we are offering a unique service, informing the public of our capabilities is of utmost importance.

Growth Strategy

After having successfully completed the entry phase into this market in the geographical area we have chosen, we will then expand our market the following ways:

1. Increase number of sales people.
2. Expand into neighboring communities.
3. Encourage word-of-mouth referrals by offering discounts.

Market Size and Share

The market for our products and services is estimated at $X billion in annual sales based on data furnished by XYZ Survey. We estimate that we can achieve a XX% market share within XX years.

Marketing data for other markets is in the process of collection.

TARGETING NEW MARKETS

To continue our growth, we will use the following methods to expand our markets and increase our new areas of business:

- Customer contact - find out their needs

- Customer referrals

- Adding additional services

- Horse shows

- Market surveys

LOCATION

This business will be operated at 123 Main Street. This location is desirable because:

- The building is structurally compatible for our use (50 box stalls).

- The rent is below market

- The building has the necessary facilities to operate this business (indoor ring and all-weather sand ring).

- The location is convenient for our customers and employees.

- Possibility of expansion in the area for more turn out paddocks.

We are renting this building on a XX year lease. Renovations costing $XXX—based upon three estimates—will be done. The building is zoned R-3, commercial use.

HISTORICAL FINANCIAL DATA

See "Attachments"

Income Statement

Sales are projected to be favorable for the next three years with a dramatic increase in year two, which is due to the implementation of an aggressive advertising campaign at the end of year one. Cost of goods sold will be reduced as well in the second quarter of year two as our inventory balances out. Selling expenses in year one will increase, due to the ad campaign; however, we expect travel & entertainment expenses to be minimal. Administrative costs will increase during the second quarter of year one, with an expected hiring of additional boarding and training staff. Year one will also have an increased rate of general expenses because of the start-up nature of the business. Overall, net income will increase to year three when the business becomes more secure in the marketplace.

Balance Sheet

We expect to remain debt-free for the first three years of business, after which we may incur a note payable to be used for improved equipment and additional real estate. Cash on hand will be minimal in order to put money back into the business and remain without debt. Accounts receivable are minimal; company policy will be primarily on a cash-only basis. However, as our customer base increases, our accounts receivable will also increase, as we will offer this billing incentive to our best customers. Inventory is to be purchased on an as-needed basis and shall fluctuate with the changing cyclical nature of the business. Products available for sale are scheduled to turn over in a four- to six-week period. Liabilities will include amounts due on inventory purchases and should fluctuate with the changing inventory needs.

We have considered seasonal trends and have forecasted accordingly. We believe the forecasts are conservative.

Cost Control

Our books will initially be maintained manually. At a future point Horses 'R' Us seeks to use a computerized accounting package to monitor our financial performance. This information will be compiled at the end of each month for preparation of financial statements. Each month these statements will be reviewed and appropriate action taken to adjust costs or our budget. If we find that we are continually over budget, our first step will be to reevaluate the markup on our products and services and to recheck our costs to be certain we are obtaining the best possible prices.

4

Business Plan Worksheets

CASH FLOW PROJECTIONS
(000s)
YEAR 1

	JAN	FEB	MAR	APR	MAY	JUN	JUL	AUG	SEP	OCT	NOV	DEC
SALES:												
Horse Sales	0.00	20.00	20.00	20.00	20.00	20.00	20.00	20.00	20.00	20.00	20.00	20.00
Home-Grown Sales (e.g., hay)	0.00	10.00	10.00	10.00	10.00	10.00	10.00	10.00	10.00	10.00	10.00	10.00
Sales	0.00	5.00	5.00	5.00	5.00	5.00	5.00	5.00	5.00	5.00	5.00	5.00
Board Income	0.00	5.00	5.00	5.00	5.00	5.00	5.00	5.00	5.00	5.00	5.00	5.00
Commissions	0.00	5.00	5.00	5.00	5.00	5.00	5.00	5.00	5.00	5.00	5.00	5.00
Leasing	0.00	5.00	5.00	5.00	5.00	5.00	5.00	5.00	5.00	5.00	5.00	5.00
Lessons/Riding-Training	0.00	5.00	5.00	5.00	5.00	5.00	5.00	5.00	5.00	5.00	5.00	5.00
Prize Money	0.00	5.00	5.00	5.00	5.00	5.00	5.00	5.00	5.00	5.00	5.00	5.00
Stud Fees	0.00	5.00	5.00	5.00	5.00	5.00	5.00	5.00	5.00	5.00	5.00	5.00
Stable Fees	0.00	5.00	5.00	5.00	5.00	5.00	5.00	5.00	5.00	5.00	5.00	5.00
Special Services	0.00	5.00	5.00	5.00	5.00	5.00	5.00	5.00	5.00	5.00	5.00	5.00
Shoeing	0.00	5.00	5.00	5.00	5.00	5.00	5.00	5.00	5.00	5.00	5.00	5.00
Braiding	0.00	5.00	5.00	5.00	5.00	5.00	5.00	5.00	5.00	5.00	5.00	5.00
Personal	0.00	5.00	5.00	5.00	5.00	5.00	5.00	5.00	5.00	5.00	5.00	5.00
Vanning	0.00	5.00	5.00	5.00	5.00	5.00	5.00	5.00	5.00	5.00	5.00	5.00
Grooming	0.00	5.00	5.00	5.00	5.00	5.00	5.00	5.00	5.00	5.00	5.00	5.00
Horse Show Fees	0.00	5.00	5.00	5.00	5.00	5.00	5.00	5.00	5.00	5.00	5.00	5.00
Registration Fees	0.00	5.00	5.00	5.00	5.00	5.00	5.00	5.00	5.00	5.00	5.00	5.00
Total Sales	0.00	110.00	110.00	110.00	110.00	110.00	110.00	110.00	110.00	110.00	110.00	110.00
CASH EXPENSES:												
Advertising	1.00	1.00	1.00	1.00	1.00	1.00	1.00	1.00	1.00	1.00	1.00	1.00
Bad Debts	0.75	0.75	0.75	0.75	0.75	0.75	0.75	0.75	0.75	0.75	0.75	0.75
Bank Charges	5.00	5.00	5.00	5.00	5.00	5.00	5.00	5.00	5.00	5.00	5.00	5.00
Board Paid Out	2.00	2.00	2.00	2.00	2.00	2.00	2.00	2.00	2.00	2.00	2.00	2.00
Bookkeeping	1.00	1.00	1.00	1.00	1.00	1.00	1.00	1.00	1.00	1.00	1.00	1.00
Building Maintenance	2.00	2.00	2.00	2.00	2.00	2.00	2.00	2.00	2.00	2.00	2.00	2.00
Charitable Contributions	2.00	2.00	2.00	2.00	2.00	2.00	2.00	2.00	2.00	2.00	2.00	2.00
Contract Services	5.00	5.00	5.00	5.00	5.00	5.00	5.00	5.00	5.00	5.00	5.00	5.00
Cost of Goods for Resale	7.00	7.00	7.00	7.00	7.00	7.00	7.00	7.00	7.00	7.00	7.00	7.00
Delivery Service	2.00	2.00	2.00	2.00	2.00	2.00	2.00	2.00	2.00	2.00	2.00	2.00
Dues	0.50	0.50	0.50	0.50	0.50	0.50	0.50	0.50	0.50	0.50	0.50	0.50
Education	1.00	1.00	1.00	1.00	1.00	1.00	1.00	1.00	1.00	1.00	1.00	1.00
Entry fees	0.20	0.20	0.20	0.20	0.20	0.20	0.20	0.20	0.20	0.20	0.20	0.20
Equipment	3.00	3.00	3.00	3.00	3.00	3.00	3.00	3.00	3.00	3.00	3.00	3.00
Farm Maintenance	0.25	0.25	0.25	0.25	0.25	0.25	0.25	0.25	0.25	0.25	0.25	0.25
Freight	1.00	1.00	1.00	1.00	1.00	1.00	1.00	1.00	1.00	1.00	1.00	1.00
Goods Damaged	0.00	1.10	1.10	1.10	1.10	1.10	1.10	1.10	1.10	1.10	1.10	1.10
Goods Donated	2.00	2.00	2.00	2.00	2.00	2.00	2.00	2.00	2.00	2.00	2.00	2.00
Goods Taken but Not Paid For	0.00	0.00	0.00	0.00	0.00	0.00	0.00	0.00	0.00	0.00	0.00	0.00
Insurance	0.00	0.00	0.00	0.00	0.00	0.00	0.00	0.00	0.00	0.00	0.00	0.00
Miscellaneous	35.00	35.00	35.00	35.00	35.00	35.00	35.00	35.00	35.00	35.00	35.00	35.00
Office Supplies	0.25	0.00	0.00	0.00	0.00	0.00	0.00	0.00	0.00	0.00	0.00	0.00
Payroll	2.00	2.00	2.00	2.00	2.00	2.00	2.00	2.00	2.00	2.00	2.00	2.00
Postage	0.20	0.00	0.00	0.00	0.00	0.00	0.00	0.00	0.00	0.00	0.00	0.00
Printing	0.00	0.00	0.00	0.00	0.00	0.00	0.00	0.00	0.00	0.00	0.00	0.00
Professional Services	1.00	0.00	0.00	0.00	0.00	0.00	0.00	0.00	0.00	0.00	0.00	0.00
Rent	2.50	2.50	2.50	2.50	2.50	2.50	2.50	2.50	2.50	2.50	2.50	2.50
Salaries (Management)	5.00	5.00	5.00	5.00	5.00	5.00	5.00	5.00	5.00	5.00	5.00	5.00
Signs	0.00	0.00	0.00	0.00	0.00	0.00	0.00	0.00	0.00	0.00	0.00	0.00
Storage Area Rent	0.00	0.00	0.00	0.00	0.00	0.00	0.00	0.00	0.00	0.00	0.00	0.00
Subscriptions	0.00	0.00	0.00	0.00	0.00	0.00	0.00	0.00	0.00	0.00	0.00	0.00
Supplies	0.00	0.00	0.00	0.00	0.00	0.00	0.00	0.00	0.00	0.00	0.00	0.00
Taxes (State, Federal, Local)	0.00	0.00	0.00	0.00	0.00	0.00	0.00	0.00	0.00	0.00	0.00	0.00
Telephone	0.75	0.75	0.75	0.75	0.75	0.75	0.75	0.75	0.75	0.75	0.75	0.75
Trailering	0.00	0.00	0.00	0.00	0.00	0.00	0.00	0.00	0.00	0.00	0.00	0.00
Training Fees	0.00	0.00	0.00	0.00	0.00	0.00	0.00	0.00	0.00	0.00	0.00	0.00
Travel & Entertainment	0.00	0.00	0.00	0.00	0.00	0.00	0.00	0.00	0.00	0.00	0.00	0.00
Utilities	0.50	0.50	0.50	0.50	0.50	0.50	0.50	0.50	0.50	0.50	0.50	0.50
Vehicle	0.50	0.00	0.00	0.00	0.00	0.00	0.00	0.00	0.00	0.00	0.00	0.00
Veterinary Fees	0.00	0.00	0.00	0.00	0.00	0.00	0.00	0.00	0.00	0.00	0.00	0.00
Total Expenses	87.90	87.05	87.05	87.05	87.05	87.05	87.05	87.05	87.05	87.05	87.05	87.05
Net Cash From Operations	-87.90	22.95	22.95	22.95	22.95	22.95	22.95	22.95	22.95	22.95	22.95	22.95
Beginning Cash	0.00	-87.90	197.05	197.05	197.05	197.05	197.05	197.05	197.05	197.05	197.05	197.05
Cash on Hand	-87.90	197.05	197.05	197.05	197.05	197.05	197.05	197.05	197.05	197.05	197.05	197.05

ASSET WORKSHEET
(000's)

Fixed Assets

Equipment	10.00
Automotive, trucks	15.00
Buildings	25.00
Fixtures	5.00
Machinery	12.00
Leasehold improvements	15.00
Start Up costs	35.00
Miscellaneous #1	0.00
Miscellaneous #2	0.00
Miscellaneous #3	0.00

Total Fixed Assets — 117.00

Intangible Assets

Goodwill	5.00
Other	0.00

Total Intangible Assets — 5.00

CASH FLOW PROJECTION WORKSHEET
(000s)

	JAN	FEB	MAR	FIRST QUARTER	APR	MAY	JUN	SECOND QUARTER
SALES:								
Horse Sales								
Home-Grown Sales (e.g., hay)								
Sales								
Board Income								
Commissions								
Leasing								
Lessons/Riding-Training								
Prize Money								
Stable Fees								
Special Services								
Shoeing								
Stud Fees								
Braiding								
Personal								
Vanning								
Grooming								
Horse Show Fees								
Registration Fees								
Other								
CASH EXPENSES:								
Advertising								
Bad Debts								
Bank Charges								
Board Paid Out								
Bookkeeping								
Building Maintenance								
Charitable Contributions								
Contract Services								
Cost of Goods for Resale								
Delivery Service								
Dues								
Education								
Entry Fees								
Equipment								
Farm Maintenance								
Freight								
Goods Damaged								
Goods Donated								
Goods Taken But Not Paid For								

CASH FLOW PROJECTION WORKSHEET (000s) - continued

	JAN	FEB	MAR	FIRST QUARTER	APR	MAY	JUN	SECOND QUARTER
Horse Purchases								
Insurance								
Miscellaneous								
Office Supplies								
Payroll								
Postage								
Printing								
Professional Services								
Rent								
Salaries (Management)								
Signs								
Storage Area Rent								
Subscriptions								
Supplies								
Bedding								
Hay								
Feed								
Other								
Telephone								
Training Fees								
Travel & Entertainment								
Utilities								
Vanning								
Vehicle								
Veterinary Fees								
Total Expenses								
Net Cash From Operations								
Beginning Cash								
Cash on Hand								
Bank Loan Required								
Loan Repayment								
Taxes (State, Federal, Local)								
Ending Cash								

CASH FLOW PROJECTION WORKSHEET
(000s)

	JUL	AUG	SEP	THIRD QUARTER	OCT	NOV	DEC	FOURTH QUARTER
SALES:								
Horse Sales								
Home-Grown Sales (e.g., hay)								
Sales								
Board Income								
Commissions								
Leasing								
Lessons/Riding-Training								
Prize Money								
Stable Fees								
Special Services								
Shoeing								
Stud Fees								
Braiding								
Personal								
Vanning								
Grooming								
Horse Show Fees								
Registration Fees								
Other								
CASH EXPENSES:								
Advertising								
Bad Debts								
Bank Charges								
Board Paid Out								
Bookkeeping								
Building Maintenance								
Charitable Contributions								
Contract Services								
Cost of Goods for Resale								
Delivery Service								
Dues								
Education								
Entry Fees								
Equipment								
Farm Maintenance								
Freight								
Goods Damaged								
Goods Donated								
Goods Taken But Not Paid For								

CASH FLOW PROJECTION WORKSHEET (000s) - continued

	JUL	AUG	SEP	THIRD QUARTER	OCT	NOV	DEC	FOURTH QUARTER
Horse Purchases								
Insurance								
Miscellaneous								
Office Supplies								
Payroll								
Postage								
Printing								
Professional Services								
Rent								
Salaries (Management)								
Signs								
Storage Area Rent								
Subscriptions								
Supplies								
Bedding								
Hay								
Feed								
Other								
Telephone								
Training Fees								
Travel & Entertainment								
Utilities								
Vanning								
Vehicle								
Veterinary Fees								
Total Expenses								
Net Cash From Operations								
Beginning Cash								
Cash on Hand								
Bank Loan Required								
Loan Repayment								
Taxes (State, Federal, Local)								
Ending Cash								

CASH FLOW PROJECTION WORKSHEET
(000s)

	Total Year		Total Year
SALES:		Horse Purchases	
Horse Sales		Insurance	
Home-Grown Sales (e.g., hay)		Miscellaneous	
Sales		Office Supplies	
Board Income		Payroll	
Commissions		Postage	
Leasing		Printing	
Lessons/Riding-Training		Professional Services	
Prize Money		Rent	
Stable Fees		Salaries (Management)	
Special Services		Signs	
Shoeing		Storage Area Rent	
Stud Fees		Subscriptions	
Braiding		Supplies	
Personal		Bedding	
Vanning		Hay	
Grooming		Feed	
Horse Show Fees		Other	
Registration Fees			
Other			
		Telephone	
		Training Fees	
		Travel & Entertainment	
		Utilities	
CASH EXPENSES:		Vanning	
Advertising		Vehicle	
Bad Debts		Veterinary Fees	
Bank Charges			
Board Paid Out		Total Expenses	
Bookkeeping			
Building Maintenance		Net Cash From Operations	
Charitable Contributions			
Contract Services		Beginning Cash	
Cost of Goods for Resale			
Delivery Service		Cash on Hand	
Dues			
Education		Bank Loan Required	
Entry Fees			
Equipment		Loan Repayment	
Farm Maintenance			
Freight		Taxes (State, Federal, Local)	
Goods Damaged			
Goods Donated		Ending Cash	
Goods Taken But Not Paid For			

QUARTERLY CASH FLOW PROJECTION WORKSHEET
(000s)

	FIRST QUARTER	SECOND QUARTER	THIRD QUARTER	FOURTH QUARTER	TOTAL YEAR
SALES:					
Horse Sales					
Home-Grown Sales (e.g., hay)					
Sales					
Board Income					
Commissions					
Leasing					
Lessons/Riding-Training					
Prize Money					
Stable Fees					
Special Services					
Shoeing					
Stud Fees					
Braiding					
Personal					
Vanning					
Grooming					
Horse Show Fees					
Registration Fees					
Other					
CASH EXPENSES:					
Advertising					
Bad Debts					
Bank Charges					
Board Paid Out					
Bookkeeping					
Building Maintenance					
Charitable Contributions					
Contract Services					
Cost of Goods for Resale					
Delivery Service					
Dues					
Education					
Entry Fees					
Equipment					
Farm Maintenance					
Freight					
Goods Damaged					
Goods Donated					
Goods Taken But Not Paid For					

QUARTERLY CASH FLOW PROJECTION WORKSHEET
(000s)

	FIRST QUARTER	SECOND QUARTER	THIRD QUARTER	FOURTH QUARTER	TOTAL YEAR
Horse Purchases					
Insurance					
Miscellaneous					
Office Supplies					
Payroll					
Postage					
Printing					
Professional Services					
Rent					
Salaries (Management)					
Signs					
Storage Area Rent					
Subscriptions					
Supplies					
Bedding					
Hay					
Feed					
Other					
Telephone					
Training Fees					
Travel & Entertainment					
Utilities					
Vanning					
Vehicle					
Veterinary Fees					
Total Expenses					
Net Cash From Operations					
Beginning Cash					
Cash on Hand					
Bank Loan Required					
Loan Repayment					
Taxes (State, Federal, Local)					
Ending Cash					

5

Bookkeeping for Horse Owners

Why Keep Records?

No horse business in today's world of sophisticated accounting can afford to operate without maintaining accurate and complete records. The following series of forms have several purposes:

    1. They provide a complete outline of all information needed by any accounting firm to draw up a financial statement and prepare all necessary tax return forms.

    2. They are evidence that may be necessary to document the profit motive of the business. If a profit motive is not recognized by the Revenue Service, then no deductions attributable to an activity will be allowed that are greater than the income generated by the activity. The Revenue Service examines the business records to determine if a profit motive exists. Inadequate accounting records reflect nonbusinesslike operations.

    3. Up-to-date records allow the taxpayer to maintain cost controls and enforce financial accountability among employees.

    4. Under the Revenue Reconciliation Act of 1993, the records are needed to substantiate that the taxpayer ''materially participates'' in his horse business to avoid passive loss limitations. (See *Tax Planning and Preparation for Horse Owners* for a complete explanation.)

Blank forms have been included in this book beginning on page 25 to assist you in documenting your active participation in the horse business.

General Advice

    1. Set up a separate bank account for the business.

    2. Keep invoices and other bills separate from personal records.

    3. Maintain depreciation schedules. (These can be determined by the accountant based on the accounting forms in this book.)

    4. Keep and preserve a file for all cancelled checks, receipts, bills, and bookkeeping records for at least six years.

Outline of Income Tax Accounting

What's Your Accounting Year?

Taxable income must be computed for a fixed period, called a taxable year. The period is usually twelve months, although a taxpayer may choose to use an annual accounting period that varies from fifty-two to fifty-three (52–53) weeks if such a period always ends on the same day of the week, the last such day of the month.

Example

A new taxpayer wishes to have his accounting period end on a Sunday. If the business came into existence on January 2, the taxpayer could choose a year beginning January 3, and ending December 25. This is a 52–53 week taxable year ending on the last Sunday of the calendar year. Alternatively, the taxpayer could elect as his first year a year ending January 1. This would be a 52–53 week taxable year ending on the Sunday nearest to the last day of the calendar year. Whichever option is chosen, it must be consistently followed.

Most taxpayers, however, adopt either a calendar or fiscal year. A fiscal year ends on the last day of any month except December. It will be recognized by the Revenue Service only if it is established as the taxpayer's annual accounting period and only if he keeps his books in accord with it. A taxpayer having no annual accounting period, or not keeping books, must compute his taxable income on a calendar-year basis.

Example

1. Riding Stable, Inc., a corporation, began doing business on Aug. 21. The end of its first tax year cannot be later than July 31, since a tax year may not cover more than a twelve-month period and must end on the last day of a month.

2. If Riding Stable, Inc., adopts the calendar-year basis, it should close its books December 31, and file its first return for the short period from August 21, through December 31. This is its first "taxable year." All its later taxable years will be full calendar years until its dissolution or unless it changes to a fiscal year.

Change of Accounting Period

A change from one accounting period to another generally requires prior permission from the Commissioner of Revenue, and always requires filing a return for the short period. Approval for a change in the accounting period is usually granted where it is established that a substantial business purpose exists for making the change. If it is determined by the Commissioner that the sole purpose of the change is to maintain or obtain a preferential tax status, approval will not be given.

Accounting Methods

The Tax Reform Act of 1987 prohibited the use of the cash method of accounting by regular corporations, partnerships that have a corporation as a partner, and tax shelters. Proposals to limit the availability of cash accounting for farmers were rejected. Horse farmers may continue to choose between the cash and accrual methods of accounting.

The owner of the horse business must decide whether to set up his records on the cash or accrual basis. In addition to having a fixed accounting period (taxable year), the taxpayer must choose one accounting method for keeping his books.

A taxpayer using the accrual method enters income into his records at the moment he has the right to receive it. It is income once it is earned, whether or not it has been collected by the taxpayer. Expenses are deducted in the year in which the amount is owed. The accrual method of accounting *must* be used when yearly inventories are necessary to reflect purchases and sales accurately.

If a payment is clearly not collectible, the taxpayer using the accrual method is not required to record the account receivable as income. If he has already included this sale in income, then he takes a bad-debt deduction to offset it.

If the taxpayer is uncertain of the liability, he should not record the expense until it is fixed and certain. If the liability is uncontested but the amount is uncertain, the taxpayer should estimate the figure and record it at that time. Any necessary adjustment can be made at a later date.

The accrual method allows the taxpayer to follow the actual ebb and flow of his finances as the income and expenses are earned or owed. Yet it does not provide the taxpayer with any flexibility in timing his profits. (See *Tax Planning and Preparation for Horse Owners,* for an explanation of planning a profit year.)

The cash basis (cash receipts and disbursements method) of accounting is the method used by most *individuals* and is still available to a horse farming business under the Tax Reform Act. Breeding, raising, training, and racing of horses are activities normally classified within the farming business, since arguably no products are being produced and sold.

The cash-basis taxpayer reports income in the year he actually receives it, either in the form of cash or other property. He deducts expenses in the year he actually pays them (although there are some restrictions on prepaid items).

The cash method normally benefits the horseman, since certain costs of breeding, raising, and training horses are deductible when paid. Under the accrual method, these costs must be added to the "basis" of the horse, as if the costs were part of the purchase price. Adding these expenses to the purchase price of the horse is called "capitalizing the costs." These costs are recovered over the useful life of the horse through depreciation (see Chapter 4).

If the horse is bought for the purpose of resale, these costs may not be recovered until the actual sale, when less profit will be recognized. In other words, under the accrual method of accounting, expenses are not recovered until the horse is put into use or sold. Under the cash method, the expenses are deductible when paid.

The accrual method is required for corporations with gross receipts over one million dollars. Family corporations and Subchapter S corporations do not fall within this rule. These small corporations may use the cash basis of accounting.

The forms presented in Chapter 8 allow you to use either accounting method. When completed, they will provide information needed to draw up a financial statement and prepare necessary tax returns, as covered more fully in the authors' *Tax Planning and Preparation for Horse Owners*.

Audit Process Relating to Records

The Revenue Service examines the taxpayer's books and records either at his place of business where these materials are kept or at an IRS office.

There may be a summons issued to a third-party recordkeeper (bank, broker, accountant) for the production of records pertaining to the business. The taxpayer must be notified of this summons also.

Warning: Keep your records, since income taxes can be assessed within three years after the original return was filed (the last day prescribed for filing if the taxpayer filed early). A proceeding to collect taxes may be begun at any time if a false return or no return was filed. If over 25% of the gross income is omitted from the return, the Revenue Service has six years to act.

6

Cash Basis Accounting

Using the Cash Basis Account Book

The cash basis account book will help you, the taxpayer, run a more efficient horse business. A good set of records is a necessity in the highly competitive commercialized business of horses today.

Legally, taxpayers have the burden of proving both a profit motive and active involvement in their business under audit. In court, taxpayers with thorough records have more often prevailed while those with incomplete, unprofessional accounts have been faced with expensive bills from the Internal Revenue Service.

Suggestions

1. Keep the book up-to-date, summarize it, and study the figures.
2. Compare the figures of your horse business with those of comparable horse operations.
3. Maintain the strong areas of your business and improve or eliminate the weak areas.
4. Use the book when planning your credit needs.

Key to Income Accounts

The income accounts are numbered to correspond with Schedule F (Farm Income and Expenses) and other applicable returns. The numbers will facilitate your own tax return preparation as well as simplify the work for your accountant.

101   "F" HORSE SALES: Income received from the sale of horses or other livestock bought by the taxpayer for *resale*. (These will be reported on Schedule F);

102   "4797" HORSE SALES: Income received from sales of horses *not bought for resale* but used in the business for draft, breeding, or sport purposes. (These will be reported on Form 4797 and on Schedule D for Capital Gains);

103   HOME GROWN SALES: Income received from the sale of horses, other livestock, or other products you raised. (These will be reported on Schedule F);

104   SALES: Other income received from the *resale of merchandise and other items* you bought for resale. (These will also be reported on Schedule F.)

Other Income

All these items will be reported as one total item on your Schedule F. The separate accounting will provide you with a planning tool and a clear "paper track" in the event questions are raised by the Internal Revenue Service.

105 BOARDING: Income received from boarding horses;

106 COMMISSIONS: Income received from horse finding activities;

107 LEASING: Income received from leasing horses;

108 LESSONS/RIDING-TRAINING FEES: Income received from students for riding lessons, horse rentals, trail rides, or for individual training sessions;

109 PRIZE MONEY: Income received in the form of cash or the equivalent value received as winnings; or for riding horses in competition for others;

110 STABLE FEES: Income received from charges for stable services such as exercise, grooming, or vitamin supplements;

112–116 INCOME RECEIVED FROM OTHER SOURCES: Set up individual accounts if regularly occurring or use the heading "Other Miscellaneous."

Key to Cash Disbursements Accounts

NOTE: Cash Disbursements Accounts have been set up to correspond to items listed as deductions on IRS Schedule F, "Farm Income and Expenses." A taxpayer is entitled to deduct all ordinary and necessary expenses of carrying on the business of farming. Breeding, raising, training, and racing of horses is normally classified as a farming business.

201 BREEDING: Incurred for breeding (stud fees);

202 CONSERVATION EXPENSES: The Tax Reform Act limits the expensing deduction to amounts consistent with a state conservation plan that will satisfy federal standards;

203 FEED PURCHASED: All feed purchased for horses or other livestock and costs for bedding stalls;

204 FERTILIZERS AND LIME: A farmer, other than a farm syndicate, may elect to deduct current expenditures otherwise chargeable to the capital account made for fertilizer, lime, ground limestone, and other materials for enriching or conditioning the land;

205 FREIGHT TRUCKING: Charges for delivery and other horse travel expenses: vanning. Do not include transportation costs related to the purchase of horses; however, these are not currently deductible expenses and should be recorded separately with the cost of purchasing the horse;

206 GASOLINE, FUEL, OIL: Costs of operating your automobile for business purposes or the horse van or truck;

207   INSURANCE: Charges for insuring property owned by the business;

208   LAND CLEARING: Under the Tax Reform Act, only routine brush clearing and ordinary maintenance activities related to property already used in farming are deductibles;

209   LABOR HIRED: All wages to employees are recorded as they are paid. Enter net pay when paid to employees, and enter amounts withheld for payment of income and social security taxes when such amounts are paid to the government. Any draw by an owner or partner must be entered under Account 229 ''Personal.'' See payroll records;

210   MACHINE HIRE: Cost of renting equipment used in the farming operation such as a mower or post hole digger;

211   MORTGAGE INTEREST: Payments made for interest charges on any business property secured by a mortgage;

212   OTHER INTEREST: Payments made for interest charges on business loans;

213   RENT OF FARM, PASTURE: Rental paid for farm land or buildings;

214   REPAIRS MAINTENANCE: Cost of any repairs made to business machinery, equipment, or the stable;

215   SUPPLIES PURCHASED: All tack and equipment purchased for operational use. Do not include merchandise purchased for resale. Cost of merchandise and horses for resale should be recorded in separate accounts;

216   TAXES: Property taxes paid on real property used in the trade or business, as are state and local taxes imposed on business income only;

217   VETERINARY FEES: Fees paid to veterinarians for horse or other livestock care, medicines, and other medical expenses;

Accounts under numbers 218–230 correspond to deductible expenses tallied on Schedule F under ''Other'':

218   ADVERTISING AND PROMOTION: Costs of promoting the business, advertising expenses or services, and gifts for good-will purposes ($25 limit per recipient);

219   BLACKSMITH: Payments to blacksmith for shoeing and supplies;

220   BOARD: Payments for boarding horses;

221   DUES & SUBSCRIPTIONS: Dues paid to professional and business associations and subscriptions to newspapers, magazines, and trade journals used in business;

222   EDUCATION: Education expenses paid to maintain or improve you in your current business. (Education to qualify you for a new business is not deductible);

223   ENTERTAINMENT & TRAVEL: Carfare, trains, buses, taxis, hotel, meal and entertainment expenses for business-related activities. The Tax Reform Act limits the deduction to 80% of your cost;

224   ENTRY FEES: Fees paid for entering horse shows, rodeos, or races;

225   LEGAL & ACCOUNTING: Legal expenses. (Including the price of this book);

226   OFFICE: All costs of operating the office, including supplies, postage, and business equipment such as adding machines, typewriters, word processors, telephone answering machines, etc.;

227   PERSONAL: Any draw by owner or partner to be used for living or family, such as personal insurance, rent, food, clothing, medical, or pleasure. This draw cannot be treated as a salary or wage earning under tax law;

228   TELEPHONE: Charges for business telephone use. If a home phone is used for business, record here only charges that apply to business; personal use is recorded under Account, ''Personal'';

229   TRAINING FEES: Fees paid for training horses;

230   OTHER: Use for miscellaneous and seldom-occurring expenses, or set up account numbers following 230 to suit individual business needs (loans, receivables, donations, etc.). If more space is needed, accounts listed above can be changed to suit your individual requirements;

301   HORSES FOR INVESTMENT OR USE: All horses or other livestock purchased for draft, sport, or breeding purposes. Do not include here horses or livestock purchased for resale. Enter each horse under this category on the Depreciation Schedule provided in this book. The yearly deduction will be determined on Form 4562;

302   HORSE FOR RESALE: All horses or other livestock purchased for resale purposes. The cost of each horse must be recorded, but it will not be deducted as a current expense. The cost of the horse must be computed to determine the basis for resale purposes.

Instructions for Completing Forms

Blank forms begin on page 26. There are 12 sets of cash forms, one set for each month. The forms are cash disbursements, income, and a monthly summary.

Cash Disbursements

1. Enter daily all disbursements (expenses) made in cash or by check. Record the corresponding account number from the Key, above, or the Monthly Summary page which follows.

2. At the end of the month, transfer the total for each expense account number to the first column ('Total This Month") of the Monthly Summary of Disbursements.

3. On the Summary, for each account add the first column to the second column, and enter the result in the last column, "Total to Date."

4. Total each column vertically. "Total Cash Disbursements This Month," from the itemized pages should equal the Summary Disbursements column "Total This Month."

5. Copy all figures from the last column of the Summary ("Total to Date") to the next month's Summary of Disbursements middle column ("Total to Last Month").

Income

1. Enter daily all income received (cash or check). Record the corresponding account number from the Key, above, or the Monthly Summary page which follows. It is a good check on your records to write in the cost or other basis of a sales horse in the "item" space.

2. At the end of the month, transfer the total for each income account number to the first column ("Total This Month") of the Monthly Summary of Income.

3. On the Summary, for each account add the first column to the second column, and enter the result in the last column, "Total to Date."

4. Total each column vertically. "Total Income This Month," from the itemized page should equal the Summary Income column, "Total This Month."

5. Copy all figures from the last column of the Summary ("Total to Date") to the next month's Summary of Income middle column ("Total to Last Month").

NOTE: The Client Account Record on page 74 may also be used by the cash-basis taxpayer.

CASH DISBURSEMENTS
CASH BASIS

Month of _February_

DATE	CHECK NO.	PAYEE	ITEM AND QUANTITY	ACCT. NO.	AMOUNT
2/3	405	Agway Hay	½ ton feed	203	85 00
2/5	406	Cantwell Training		229	550 00
2/6	407	Mc Brien Stables	purchased "_____"	302	1490 00
2/6	"	"	transp. of "_____"	205	100 00
2/12	408	Feeger	3 tons bedding	203	300 00
2/14	409	Mid Island Shows	entry fee "_____"	301	45 00
2/15	410	Birdsall Farrier	shoeing 6 @ $65	219	390 00
2/15	411	Golding Suppliers	stall door	215	75 00
2/17	412	Cedar Farm Stud	for "_____"	201	750 00
2/18	413	Swan Creek Stable	board "_____"	220	425 00
2/18	414	Janet McBrien	training "_____"	229	25 00
2/19	415	E.H. Vet. Group	for "_____"	217	175 00
2/19	416	N.Y. Tel. Co.		228	85 15
2/19	417	Pretl CPA		225	100 00
2/23	418	Jeannette Schwenk	Commission for "_____"	230	1500 00
2/28	419	Al Giaquinto	Net Paid (after deductions)	201	342 70
			TOTAL CASH DISBURSEMENTS THIS MONTH		19847 85

INCOME
CASH BASIS

Month of _February_

DATE OF DEPOSIT	CHECK NO.	RECEIVED FROM	ACCT. NO.	AMOUNT	DATE OF DEPOSIT	CHECK NO.	RECEIVED FROM	ACCT. NO.	AMOUNT
							TOTAL FORWARDED		12355 00
2/3	843	Olsen Stables	110	800 00					
"	401	John Smith	101	375 00	2/25	cash	Rich Lynch	103	10 00
"	1101	Al Brown	101	375 00	"	cash	P. Leslie	103	10 00
"	"	"	102	125 00	"	382	M. O'Donnell	104	35 00
2/7	1343	Boyce, Ltd.	111	750 00	"	1343	French Farms (Red)	110	1000 00
"	cash	Alan Goodstein	103	10 00	"	2401	Nichols Stables	101	400 00
2/14	121	Peg Jackson	110	1800 00	"	420	Tina Smith	103	10 00
"	8741	Stedding Stables	107	7500 00	2/28	1435	Peter South (Sunny)	108	500 00
"	591	Joyce Carter	104	35 00					
2/21	204	Mid-Islander Shows	109	150 00					
"	974	R. Russo	104	200 00					
"	409	Tina Smith	106	200 00					
"	378	M. O'Donnell	104	35 00					
		TOTAL FORWARD		12355 00			**TOTAL INCOME THIS MONTH**		14320 00

MONTHLY SUMMARY
CASH BASIS

Month of _February_

ACCT. NO.	ACCOUNT (INCOME)	TOTAL THIS MONTH	TOTAL TO LAST MONTH	TOTAL TO DATE	ACCT. NO.	ACCOUNT (DISBURSEMENTS)	TOTAL THIS MONTH	TOTAL TO LAST MONTH	TOTAL TO DATE
101	"F" Horse Sales	1,800 00		1,800 00	201	Breeding	500 00	250 00	750 00
102	"4797" Horse Sales	2,600 00	800 00	3,400 00	202	Conservation	620 00		620 00
103	Home-Grown Sales	1,500 00	500 00	2,000 00	203	Feed Purchased	1,400 00	1,300 00	2,700 00
104	Sales	7,500 00		7,500 00	204	Fertilizers and Lime			
105	Boarding	1,150 00	950 00	2,100 00	205	Freight Trucking	100 00	75 00	175 00
106	Commission	750 00		750 00	206	Gas, Fuel, Oil	50 00	65 00	115 00
107	Leasing	200 00		200 00	207	Insurance	750 00		750 00
108	Lessons/Riding-Training	105 00	85 00	190 00	208	Land Clearing			
109	Prize Money	150 00		150 00	209	Labor Hired	400 00	400 00	800 00
110	Stable Fees	125 00	200 00	325 00	210	Machine Hire	85 00	25 00	110 00
111	Other-Miscellaneous	40 00	70 00	110 00	211	Mortgage Interest	125 00	125 00	250 00
112	Other-Shoeing				212	Other Interest			
113	Other-Braiding		40 00	40 00	213	Rent of Farm	1,000 00	1,000 00	2,000 00
114	Other-Personal				214	Repairs Maintenance	60 00	170 00	230 00
115	Other-Grooming				215	Supplies Purchased	135 00		135 00
116	Other-Breeding Income	1,000 00	750 00	1,750 00	216	Taxes			
117					217	Veterinary Fees	325 00	50 00	375 00
118					218	Advertising	75 00	75 00	150 00
119					219	Blacksmith	425 00	375 00	800 00
120					220	Board	625 00	625 00	1250 00
121					221	Dues & Subscriptions			
					222	Education			
	TOTAL THIS MONTH	16,920 00			223	Entertainment & Travel			
	TOTAL TO LAST MONTH		3,395 00		224	Entry Fees			
					225	Legal & Accounting	600 00		600 00
					226	Office	250 00	325 00	575 00
	TOTAL TO DATE			20,315 00	227	Personal			
					228	Telephone	85 00	105 00	190 00
					229	Training/Transportation of Horse	350 00		350 00

PROFIT AND (LOSS)

Total Income This Month	16,920.00
Less Total Disb. This Month	10,960.00
Profit (Loss) This Month	5,960.00
Total Income To Date	20,315.00
Less Total Disb. To Date	18,425.00
Profit (Loss) To Date	1,890.00

ACCT. NO.	ACCOUNT	TOTAL THIS MONTH	TOTAL TO LAST MONTH	TOTAL TO DATE
230	Other			
301	Horses for Investment or Use	3,000 00		3,000 00
302	Horses for Resale		2,500	2,500 00
	TOTAL THIS MONTH	10,960 00		
	TOTAL TO LAST MONTH		7,465 00	
	TOTAL TO DATE			18,425 00

7

Accrual Basis Accounting

Using the Accrual Basis Account Book

As discussed in Chapter 1, under the accrual method of accounting, expenses are deductible in the year when all the events have occurred that fix the amount of the expense item and determine the liability of the taxpayer to pay it. Income should be entered in the records when there is a right to receive it, even if it is not actually received until a later date. The blank forms are available beginning on page 75.

Instructions for Completing Forms

AccountsReceivable
(includes Client Account Record, Sales Journal, and Cash Receipts forms)

1. As a client is invoiced, record the total amount due in the Credit column of the appropriate individual Client Account Record.

2. Record the same amount in the Accounts Receivable (A) column of the Sales Journal, and the breakdown in the appropriate columns (B-F). Col. A = Col. B + Col. C + Col. D + Col. E + Col. F.

3. When payment is received, in cash or by check, record the amount deposited in Column A of the Cash Receipts form and the breakdown in the appropriate columns to the right (B and C). Col. A = Cols. B + Col. C.

4. At the same time, record the payment as a debit in the appropriate Client Account Record.

Accounts Payable
(includes Accounts Payable and Cash Disbursements forms)

1. When a debt is *incurred* (not necessarily when it is paid), record the amount due in Column A of the Accounts Payable form, along with the name of the vendor. These are your accrued expenses. Record the item description and amount in the appropriate columns to the right (B and C). Col. A = Cols. B + C.

2. When you make a payment, in cash or by check, record the amount in Columns A through E of the Cash Disbursements form, and the breakdown in the appropriate columns to the right (F-I). Cols. A + B + C + D + E = Cols. F + G + H + I.

Monthly Reconciliation

1. Total all forms.

2. The total Balance Due of all Client Account Records is your outstanding accounts receivable. This should equal the total Accounts Receivable column (Col. A) of the Sales Journal *minus* the total Accounts Receivable column (Col. B) of the Cash Receipts.

3. Your outstanding accounts payable is the total Accounts Payable column (Col. A) of Accounts Payable *minus* the total Net Check column (Col. A) of Cash Disbursements.

8

Deductible Expenses and Depreciation

Deductible Expenses

One of the selling points of investing in the horse business has been favorable cost-recovery methods under past tax laws. As a legitimate tax shelter, losses from a business with a profit motive were fully deductible against other income.

Under the Tax Reform Act of 1986, such deductions became subject to the passive loss limitations. The new law provides that a taxpayer must "materially participate" in the business in order to apply losses from his horse business against his salary, active business income, or even to offset his portfolio income. Losses and credits from a passive non-participatory horse business investment would only be deductible against other passive income. Losses which are not currently allowed can be carried forward indefinitely and used in subsequent years to offset passive income. What all this means to the horse owner is clear. He must keep careful records to demonstrate his involvement in the daily operations of the business and to document his active role in management. This provision is discussed more fully in the companion edition, *Tax Planning and Preparation for Horse Owners*. The importance of on-going records to prove active participation cannot be underestimated this year. An individual must meet the requirements of at least one of several tests if he is to fully deduct losses from the horse business each year.

Tests for Proving Active Participation

While the tests are fully explained in the companion book, the important issue here is to maintain a consistent regular method of recording your time spent. If you are asked to prove you are an active participant who has "earned" her losses, the time charts will be invaluable.

What must you prove?

1. You spent more than 500 hours during the year; or

2. You spent more than 100 hours during the year and no one else (including employees) spent more time; or

3. You spent more than 500 hours during the year on various activities but no less than 100 on any one particular aspect of the business; or

4. You participated on a regular, continuous, and substantial basis during the year *and* spent at least 100 hours.

Use the journal on page 19 to jot down your activities. Don't make up "busy work." If you pay a manager, don't chalk up management hours. As an investor, the time you spend analyzing your financial reports will not count.

At Risk Limitations

The amount of loss that may be deducted in connection with a farming activity cannot exceed the total amount the taxpayer has "at risk" in that activity at the close of the year. The amount "at risk" includes cash, the basis of property contributed, and any amount borrowed for which the taxpayer is personally liable. A buyer is not at risk if he/she buys an interest in a horse and the original owner retains an interest in the horse. If a loss is not allowed, it may be carried forward to the next tax year.

Depreciation

Horse owners and breeders in business for profit are allowed to deduct depreciation (recover the cost) of racehorses, show horses, and breeding horses, as well as farm buildings and farm machinery. Depreciation begins when the property is "placed into service" in the business—not when it is purchased or otherwise acquired. The amount of the annual depreciation is the cost of the animal or other property allocated and deducted over its recovery period. Horses that have been raised cannot be depreciated if the cost of breeding and raising them has already been deducted as an expense. Also, horses held primarily for sale cannot be depreciated. School horses are depreciable. Sale inventory stock are not. You should document the purpose and primary uses of your horses.

Under the Tax Reform Act, the cost of horses is recovered over either a three-year or seven-year period. The cost of racehorses more than two years old and other horses more than twelve years old are recovered over three years. This system views property as placed in service in the middle of the first year. In practical terms, the taxpayer must wait an extra year to recover the cost, thus extending three-year property to four years and seven-year property to eight years. These rules are mandatory. The taxpayer who does not depreciate loses money, since his basis is lowered as if he calculated his cost recovery. At the time he sells the horse, he must recognize a greater profit (or a smaller loss), even if he did not use his depreciation deductions.

For example, a school horse bought for $5,000 is sold for $4,000. the stable owner files, claiming a $1,000 loss. Sorry, he has, in fact, a $1,500 gain from the point of view of the IRS. The owner failed to take the appropriate depreciation deductions on his past returns of $2,500. That is his error, not to be recouped. Therefore, when the horse was sold for $4,000, the depreciated basis of $2,500 is the starting point, not the original $5,000.

Depreciation for property in the 3, 5, 7, 10, 15, and 20-year classes is calculated using the declining balance method of computation at the rate of 150%, one and one-half times the straight-line rate.·

In contrast, the nonresidential property (i.e., the stable) is the big loser. It must be depreciated over 39 years, using the straight-line method. (For complete discussion of depreciation, see the companion edition, *Tax Planning and Preparation for Horse Owners*.)

Cost Recovery Schedules

The percentages for the latest changes are based on the mathematical application of the prescribed 150% declining balance method.

1. Racehorses more than two years old and other horses more than twelve years old:

Year in Service	Percent of Cost or Other Basis Allowed (150% rate) for property used in trade or business of farming
1	25.00%
2	37.50%
3	25.00%
4	12.50%
	100.00%

The first-year cost-recovery rate applies regardless of when during the year the horse is placed into service.

This schedule also applies to light-duty trucks and automobiles if they are used in connection with the business.

2. Other Horses and Equipment:

Year in Service	Percent of Cost or Other Basis Allowed (150% rate) for property used in trade or business of farming
1	10.71%
2	19.13%
3	15.03%
4	12.25%
5	12.25%
6	12.25%
7	12.25%
8	6.25%
	100.00%

This schedule also applies to all farm equipment, machinery, fencing, and single-purpose or agricultural structures except general-purpose farm buildings. Again, the percentages apply regardless of when during the year the property is placed into service, unless there is a short tax year.

3. Buildings: Farm buildings are depreciated over a 39 year period using straight-line depreciation.

4. Used Property: The above schedules apply to all used property as well as to new property. (See *Tax Planning and Preparation for Horse Owners* for a more complete discussion.)

Half-Year Convention

Under MACRS, the taxpayer must treat the property as placed into service on July 1, in effect adding a year to the schedules. If the horse is purchased and begins use in May, the buyer counts from July 1, and the period will not end until July 1, four years later, If more than 40% of the cost of property is placed into service during the last quarter of the tax year, a mid-quarterly convention must be applied to all property placed into service during the year.

The mid-quarter convention deems property placed into service during a particular quarter as having been placed into service on the midpoint of that quarter. The effect of this midpoint is as follows:

Property placed in service		Percentage Allowed
1st Quarter — 7/8	x	appropriate percentage for year
2nd Quarter — 5/8	x	appropriate percentage for year
3rd Quarter — 3/8	x	appropriate percentage for year
4th Quarter — 1/8	x	appropriate percentage for year

The taxpayer who feels overwhelmed by these details is advised to maintain the depreciation schedule on the next page. You will have all the necessary information for any professional tax return preparer.

Exclusion

Horses or other property used predominantly outside the United States are depreciated over a longer period, under another set of rules using straight-line depreciation.

Instructions for Depreciation Schedule

To calculate depreciation, the taxpayer needs to determine: 1) the tax basis, and 2) whether the basis is recoverable over three, five, seven, or more years. For a horse business, the original tax basis is generally the cost plus additional fees related to the purchase which were not currently deductible. See page 79 for the blank form.

The cost-recovery schedules above will give you the recovery period for the various classes of property which will then allow you to complete the Depreciation Schedule. This Depreciation Schedule corresponds to the IRS Form 4562, "Depreciation and Amortization."

Your basis column for purposes of calculating depreciation remains the same through the life of the property. For resale or trade purpose, the basis is the original cost or other basis less any depreciation taken in previous years.

DEPRECIATION SCHEDULE

Year_____   ACCRUAL OR CASH BASIS

A	B	C	D	E	F	G
Description of Property	Date Placed in Service	Cost or Other Basis	Depreciation Allowed or Allowable in Prior Years	Method	Life or Rate	Deduction This Year
Tackroom Fixtures and Equipment	Jan., 1981	$3,000	$321	Str. Line	10 yr.	$300
School Horse	Jan., 1990	$3,500	$0	MACRS	7 yr.	$525
Truck/Van	Mar., 1986	$12,750	$2,550	Str. Line	7 yr.	$2,550

ACTIVE PARTICIPATION JOURNAL		
Date	**Brief Description of Activity**	**Time***
1/03	Planned yearly horse show schedule	1.0
1/06	Made reservations for Tampa show and interviewed two groom applicants	1.2
1/08	Attended horse show and videoed performance of potential purchase horse	2.3
1/12	Conference with trainer setting year's objectives and solving problems of stable space.	2.0
1/25	Negotiated sale of show jumper and bought new hunter from Smith Inc.	3.0
	TOTAL:	11.5

*Based on .1 = 6 minutes, 1.0 = 1 hour
If you are to accumulate the minimum 100 hours per year, you need 8 hours and 20 minutes a month.
Suggestion: Copy the journal form and maintain one for each month.

Question: What must I do to materially participate in the business activity?

Answer: Spend more than 500 hours per year in a particular business activity. If you spend fewer than 500 hours and more than 100 hours per year, you can qualify if the facts and circumstances show you participated on a regular, substantial, and continuous basis. Keep your journal up-to-date.

Question: Will my different business operations be considered as separate business activities?

Answer: There is an "aggregation rule" which allows a person to consider all the business operations at a single location as one undertaking. Also, several businesses that are similar and controlled by the same person or persons will be considered as one, even if the locations are different. Again, keep your journal up-to-date and clearly labeled.

See page 80 for the blank form, Active Participation Journal.

9

Payroll Records

Compliance

An employer is responsible for filing proper forms, as well as withholding taxes on behalf of its employees and periodically remitting such taxes to the government. Call the Internal Revenue Service or your State employment office to obtain a list of required forms to be filed and the correct taxes to be withheld. See new rules and discussion in *Tax Planning and Preparation for Horse Owners*.

Certain types of wages in the past were specifically excluded from "wage for income-tax withholding purposes." Agricultural labor, which includes breeding and raising horses for sale, is no longer exempt from withholding. Penalties for not complying can be severe.

Instructions for Completing Forms

How often you are required to remit to the government the amounts you have withheld depends on how much any period you have withheld on behalf of all employees. The timing of payment is triggered by the size of your payroll. Up-to-date records are a must. Blank forms are available on page 81.

1. Each pay period, record the employee's wages earned as regular salary and/or overtime, and the total gross wages, in the appropriate columns on each "Individual Payroll Record." Record all amounts withheld and the "Net Pay" for that pay period.

2. On the "Master Payroll Record," enter the "Gross Wages for All Employees" as well as the total withholding for all employees.

3. At the end of each quarter, total all columns for that quarter on both "individual" and "Master Payroll Records." Add the total for the current quarter to those of previous quarters to figure "Year-to-Date" totals.

10

Horse Record

Keeping an individual record of each horse will be useful to a business using either accrual-or cash-basis accounting. Make copies of the blank form, "Horse Record," on page 22 for your convenience to be clipped into a looseleaf notebook, filed alphabetically under the horse's name or chronologically by the date of purchase.

HORSE RECORD
ACCRUAL OR CASH BASIS

Name Of Horse: _____
Description: _____
Purchase Price: _____
Purchased From: _____
Date of Purchase: _____

Additional expense at purchase: _____

Total cost of horse: _____

DATE	EXPLANATION	TACK & EQUIPMENT	VETERINARY/ MEDICINES	BLACKSMITHS	VANNING	RENT OR BOARD	ENTRY FEES	TRAINING FEES	ADVERTISING/ PROMOTION	OTHER

11

Financial Statement

FINANCIAL STATEMENT
(Statement of Net Worth)
Year _____

Assets	Value	Liabilities	Value
1. Cash on hand	$	1. Notes payable:	
2. Cash in bank (balance)	....	....	$ ....
3. Loans receivable, secured	....	....	....
4. Loans receivable, unsecured	....	....	....
5. Accounts receivable	....	....	....
6. Cash value of insurance policies	....	....	....
7. Stocks and bonds	....	2. Accounts payable:	
8. United States securities	....	....	....
9. Livestock: a) Show horses	....	....	....
b) Breeding horses	....	....	....
c) Racing horses	....	....	....
d) Sales horses	....	....	....
e) Other	....	3. Insurance premiums, past due	....
f) Other	....	4. Interest past due	....
10. Feed on hand	....	5. Taxes, delinquent	....
11. Tack or equipment for sale	....	6. Other current liabilities	....
....	....	....	....
12. Other quick assets	....	....	....
....	....	....	....
13. Current assets, Total	$	....	....
14. Farm real estate	....	7. Current Liabilities, Total	$ ....
....	....	8. Real estate mortgage	....
....	....	9. Other mortgages of liens	....
....	....	....	....
....	....	....	....
15. Other real estate	....	10. Judgement and other liens	....
16. Farm machinery and equipment	....	11. Other deferred liabilities	....
17. Other fixed assets	....	....	....
....	....	....	....
....	....	12. Liabilities, Total (lines 7 and up to 12) .	....
....	....	13. Net worth (Assets minus Liabilities	$ _____
18. Assets, Total (lines 13 and up to 18)	$	14. Totals (line 12 plus line 13)	$ ....

NET WORTH SUMMARY

Item	Beginning Of Year	End Of Year	Change During Year
Assets, total	$	$	$ ....
Liabilities, total	$	$	$ ....
NET WORTH	$	$	$

12

Blank Forms

Cash Disbursements (Cash Method)
Income
Monthly Summary
Client Account Record
Sales Journal
Cash Receipts
Accounts Payable
Cash Disbursements (Accrual Method)
Depreciation Schedule
Active Participation Journal
Individual Payroll Record
Master Payroll Record

CASH DISBURSEMENTS
CASH BASIS

Month of _____

DATE	CHECK NO.	PAYEE	ITEM & QUANTITY	ACCT. NO.	AMOUNT	
				TOTAL FORWARD		

CASH DISBURSEMENTS (continued)

Month of _____

DATE	CHECK NO.	PAYEE	ITEM & QUANTITY	ACCT. NO.	AMOUNT	
			TOTAL FORWARDED			
			TOTAL CASH DISBURSEMENTS THIS MONTH			

INCOME
CASH BASIS

Month of _____,

DATE OF DEPOSIT	CHECK NO.	RECEIVED FROM	ACCT. NO.	AMOUNT		DATE OF DEPOSIT	CHECK NO.	RECEIVED FROM	ACCT. NO.	AMOUNT	
				TOTAL FORWARD			*TOTAL INCOME THIS MONTH*				

MONTHLY SUMMARY
CASH BASIS

Month of _____

INCOME

ACCT. NO.	ACCOUNT	TOTAL THIS MONTH		TOTAL TO LAST MONTH		TOTAL TO DATE	
101	"F" Horse Sales						
102	"4797" Horse Sales						
103	Home-Grown Sales						
104	Sales						
105	Boarding						
106	Commission						
107	Leasing						
108	Lessons/Riding-Training						
109	Prize Money						
110	Stable Fees						
111	Other - Miscellaneous						
112	Other - Shoeing						
113	Other - Braiding						
114	Other - Personal						
115	Other - Grooming						
116	Other - Breeding Income						
117							
118							
119							
120							
121							
Total This Month							
Total To Last Month							
Total To Date							

DISBURSEMENTS

ACCT. NO.	ACCOUNT	TOTAL THIS MONTH		TOTAL TO LAST MONTH		TOTAL TO DATE	
201	Breeding						
202	Conservation						
203	Feed Purchased						
204	Fertilizer and Lime						
205	Freight Trucking						
206	Gas, Fuel, Oil						
207	Insurance						
208	Land Clearing						
209	Labor Hired						
210	Machine Hire						
211	Mortgage Interest						
212	Other Interest						
213	Rent of Farm						
214	Repairs Maintenance						
215	Supplies Purchased						
216	Taxes						
217	Veterinary Fees						
218	Advertising						
219	Blacksmith						
220	Board						
221	Dues & Subscriptions						
222	Education						
223	Entertainment & Travel						
224	Entry Fees						
225	Legal & Accounting						
226	Office						
227	Personal						
228	Telephone						
229	Training/Transportation of Horse						
230	Other						
301	Horse for Investment or Use						
301	Horse for Resale						
TOTAL THIS MONTH							
TOTAL TO LAST MONTH							
TOTAL TO DATE							

PROFIT AND (LOSS)

Total Income This Month _____

Less Total Disbursements This Month _____

Profit (Loss) This Month _____

Total Income To Date _____

Less Total Disbursements To Date _____

Profit (Loss) To Date _____

CASH DISBURSEMENTS
CASH BASIS

Month of _____

DATE	CHECK NO.	PAYEE	ITEM & QUANTITY	ACCT. NO.	AMOUNT	
				TOTAL FORWARD		

CASH DISBURSEMENTS (continued)

Month of _____

DATE	CHECK NO.	PAYEE	ITEM & QUANTITY	ACCT. NO.	AMOUNT	
			TOTAL FORWARDED			
			TOTAL CASH DISBURSEMENTS THIS MONTH			

INCOME
CASH BASIS

Month of _____

DATE OF DEPOSIT	CHECK NO.	RECEIVED FROM	ACCT. NO.	AMOUNT		DATE OF DEPOSIT	CHECK NO.	RECEIVED FROM	ACCT. NO.	AMOUNT	
			TOTAL FORWARD					*TOTAL INCOME THIS MONTH*			

MONTHLY SUMMARY
CASH BASIS

Month of _____

INCOME

ACCT. NO.	ACCOUNT	TOTAL THIS MONTH		TOTAL TO LAST MONTH		TOTAL TO DATE	
101	"F" Horse Sales						
102	"4797" Horse Sales						
103	Home-Grown Sales						
104	Sales						
105	Boarding						
106	Commission						
107	Leasing						
108	Lessons/Riding-Training						
109	Prize Money						
110	Stable Fees						
111	Other - Miscellaneous						
112	Other - Shoeing						
113	Other - Braiding						
114	Other - Personal						
115	Other - Grooming						
116	Other - Breeding Income						
117							
118							
119							
120							
121							
Total This Month							
Total To Last Month							
Total To Date							

PROFIT AND (LOSS)

Total Income This Month _____

Less Total Disbursements This Month _____

Profit (Loss) This Month _____

Total Income To Date _____

Less Total Disbursements To Date _____

Profit (Loss) To Date _____

DISBURSEMENTS

ACCT. NO.	ACCOUNT	TOTAL THIS MONTH		TOTAL TO LAST MONTH		TOTAL TO DATE	
201	Breeding						
202	Conservation						
203	Feed Purchased						
204	Fertilizer and Lime						
205	Freight Trucking						
206	Gas, Fuel, Oil						
207	Insurance						
208	Land Clearing						
209	Labor Hired						
210	Machine Hire						
211	Mortgage Interest						
212	Other Interest						
213	Rent of Farm						
214	Repairs Maintenance						
215	Supplies Purchased						
216	Taxes						
217	Veterinary Fees						
218	Advertising						
219	Blacksmith						
220	Board						
221	Dues & Subscriptions						
222	Education						
223	Entertainment & Travel						
224	Entry Fees						
225	Legal & Accounting						
226	Office						
227	Personal						
228	Telephone						
229	Training/Transportation of Horse						
230	Other						
301	Horse for Investment or Use						
301	Horse for Resale						
TOTAL THIS MONTH							
TOTAL TO LAST MONTH							
TOTAL TO DATE							

CASH DISBURSEMENTS

Month of _____ CASH BASIS

DATE	CHECK NO.	PAYEE	ITEM & QUANTITY	ACCT. NO.	AMOUNT	
			TOTAL FORWARD			

CASH DISBURSEMENTS *(continued)*

Month of _____

DATE	CHECK NO.	PAYEE	ITEM & QUANTITY	ACCT. NO.	AMOUNT	
			TOTAL FORWARDED			
			TOTAL CASH DISBURSEMENTS THIS MONTH			

INCOME
CASH BASIS

Month of _____

DATE OF DEPOSIT	CHECK NO.	RECEIVED FROM	ACCT. NO.	AMOUNT		DATE OF DEPOSIT	CHECK NO.	RECEIVED FROM	ACCT. NO.	AMOUNT	
			TOTAL FORWARD					*TOTAL INCOME THIS MONTH*			

MONTHLY SUMMARY
CASH BASIS

Month of _____

INCOME

ACCT. NO.	ACCOUNT	TOTAL THIS MONTH		TOTAL TO LAST MONTH		TOTAL TO DATE	
101	"F" Horse Sales						
102	"4797" Horse Sales						
103	Home-Grown Sales						
104	Sales						
105	Boarding						
106	Commission						
107	Leasing						
108	Lessons/Riding-Training						
109	Prize Money						
110	Stable Fees						
111	Other - Miscellaneous						
112	Other - Shoeing						
113	Other - Braiding						
114	Other - Personal						
115	Other - Grooming						
116	Other - Breeding Income						
117							
118							
119							
120							
121							
Total This Month							
Total To Last Month							
Total To Date							

DISBURSEMENTS

ACCT. NO.	ACCOUNT	TOTAL THIS MONTH		TOTAL TO LAST MONTH		TOTAL TO DATE	
201	Breeding						
202	Conservation						
203	Feed Purchased						
204	Fertilizer and Lime						
205	Freight Trucking						
206	Gas, Fuel, Oil						
207	Insurance						
208	Land Clearing						
209	Labor Hired						
210	Machine Hire						
211	Mortgage Interest						
212	Other Interest						
213	Rent of Farm						
214	Repairs Maintenance						
215	Supplies Purchased						
216	Taxes						
217	Veterinary Fees						
218	Advertising						
219	Blacksmith						
220	Board						
221	Dues & Subscriptions						
222	Education						
223	Entertainment & Travel						
224	Entry Fees						
225	Legal & Accounting						
226	Office						
227	Personal						
228	Telephone						
229	Training/Transportation of Horse						
230	Other						
301	Horse for Investment or Use						
301	Horse for Resale						
TOTAL THIS MONTH							
TOTAL TO LAST MONTH							
TOTAL TO DATE							

PROFIT AND (LOSS)

Total Income This Month _____

Less Total Disbursements This Month _____

Profit (Loss) This Month _____

Total Income To Date _____

Less Total Disbursements To Date _____

Profit (Loss) To Date _____

CASH DISBURSEMENTS
CASH BASIS

Month of _____

DATE	CHECK NO.	PAYEE	ITEM & QUANTITY	ACCT. NO.	AMOUNT	
				TOTAL FORWARD		

CASH DISBURSEMENTS *(continued)*

Month of _____

DATE	CHECK NO.	PAYEE	ITEM & QUANTITY	ACCT. NO.	AMOUNT	
			TOTAL FORWARDED			
			TOTAL CASH DISBURSEMENTS THIS MONTH			

INCOME
CASH BASIS

Month of _____

DATE OF DEPOSIT	CHECK NO.	RECEIVED FROM	ACCT. NO.	AMOUNT		DATE OF DEPOSIT	CHECK NO.	RECEIVED FROM	ACCT. NO.	AMOUNT	
				TOTAL FORWARD				*TOTAL INCOME THIS MONTH*			

MONTHLY SUMMARY
CASH BASIS

Month of _____

INCOME

ACCT. NO.	ACCOUNT	TOTAL THIS MONTH		TOTAL TO LAST MONTH		TOTAL TO DATE	
101	"F" Horse Sales						
102	"4797" Horse Sales						
103	Home-Grown Sales						
104	Sales						
105	Boarding						
106	Commission						
107	Leasing						
108	Lessons/Riding-Training						
109	Prize Money						
110	Stable Fees						
111	Other - Miscellaneous						
112	Other - Shoeing						
113	Other - Braiding						
114	Other - Personal						
115	Other - Grooming						
116	Other - Breeding Income						
117							
118							
119							
120							
121							
	Total This Month						
	Total To Last Month						
	Total To Date						

DISBURSEMENTS

ACCT. NO.	ACCOUNT	TOTAL THIS MONTH		TOTAL TO LAST MONTH		TOTAL TO DATE	
201	Breeding						
202	Conservation						
203	Feed Purchased						
204	Fertilizer and Lime						
205	Freight Trucking						
206	Gas, Fuel, Oil						
207	Insurance						
208	Land Clearing						
209	Labor Hired						
210	Machine Hire						
211	Mortgage Interest						
212	Other Interest						
213	Rent of Farm						
214	Repairs Maintenance						
215	Supplies Purchased						
216	Taxes						
217	Veterinary Fees						
218	Advertising						
219	Blacksmith						
220	Board						
221	Dues & Subscriptions						
222	Education						
223	Entertainment & Travel						
224	Entry Fees						
225	Legal & Accounting						
226	Office						
227	Personal						
228	Telephone						
229	Training/Transportation of Horse						
230	Other						
301	Horse for Investment or Use						
301	Horse for Resale						
	TOTAL THIS MONTH						
	TOTAL TO LAST MONTH						
	TOTAL TO DATE						

PROFIT AND (LOSS)

Total Income This Month _____

Less Total Disbursements This Month _____

Profit (Loss) This Month _____

Total Income To Date _____

Less Total Disbursements To Date _____

Profit (Loss) To Date _____

CASH DISBURSEMENTS
CASH BASIS

Month of _____

DATE	CHECK NO.	PAYEE	ITEM & QUANTITY	ACCT. NO.	AMOUNT	
					TOTAL FORWARD	

CASH DISBURSEMENTS (continued)

Month of _____

DATE	CHECK NO.	PAYEE	ITEM & QUANTITY	ACCT. NO.	AMOUNT	
			TOTAL FORWARDED			
				TOTAL CASH DISBURSEMENTS THIS MONTH		

INCOME
CASH BASIS

Month of _____

DATE OF DEPOSIT	CHECK NO.	RECEIVED FROM	ACCT. NO.	AMOUNT		DATE OF DEPOSIT	CHECK NO.	RECEIVED FROM	ACCT. NO.	AMOUNT	
			TOTAL FORWARD					*TOTAL INCOME THIS MONTH*			

MONTHLY SUMMARY
CASH BASIS

Month of _____

INCOME

ACCT. NO.	ACCOUNT	TOTAL THIS MONTH		TOTAL TO LAST MONTH		TOTAL TO DATE	
101	"F" Horse Sales						
102	"4797" Horse Sales						
103	Home-Grown Sales						
104	Sales						
105	Boarding						
106	Commission						
107	Leasing						
108	Lessons/Riding-Training						
109	Prize Money						
110	Stable Fees						
111	Other - Miscellaneous						
112	Other - Shoeing						
113	Other - Braiding						
114	Other - Personal						
115	Other - Grooming						
116	Other - Breeding Income						
117							
118							
119							
120							
121							
	Total This Month						
	Total To Last Month						
	Total To Date						

DISBURSEMENTS

ACCT. NO.	ACCOUNT	TOTAL THIS MONTH		TOTAL TO LAST MONTH		TOTAL TO DATE	
201	Breeding						
202	Conservation						
203	Feed Purchased						
204	Fertilizer and Lime						
205	Freight Trucking						
206	Gas, Fuel, Oil						
207	Insurance						
208	Land Clearing						
209	Labor Hired						
210	Machine Hire						
211	Mortgage Interest						
212	Other Interest						
213	Rent of Farm						
214	Repairs Maintenance						
215	Supplies Purchased						
216	Taxes						
217	Veterinary Fees						
218	Advertising						
219	Blacksmith						
220	Board						
221	Dues & Subscriptions						
222	Education						
223	Entertainment & Travel						
224	Entry Fees						
225	Legal & Accounting						
226	Office						
227	Personal						
228	Telephone						
229	Training/Transportation of Horse						
230	Other						
301	Horse for Investment or Use						
301	Horse for Resale						
	TOTAL THIS MONTH						
	TOTAL TO LAST MONTH						
	TOTAL TO DATE						

PROFIT AND (LOSS)

Total Income This Month _____

Less Total Disbursements This Month _____

Profit (Loss) This Month _____

Total Income To Date _____

Less Total Disbursements To Date _____

Profit (Loss) To Date _____

CASH DISBURSEMENTS

CASH BASIS

Month of _____

DATE	CHECK NO.	PAYEE	ITEM & QUANTITY	ACCT. NO.	AMOUNT	
			TOTAL FORWARD			

CASH DISBURSEMENTS (continued)

Month of _____

DATE	CHECK NO.	PAYEE	ITEM & QUANTITY	ACCT. NO.	AMOUNT	
			TOTAL FORWARDED			
				TOTAL CASH DISBURSEMENTS THIS MONTH		

INCOME
CASH BASIS

Month of _____

DATE OF DEPOSIT	CHECK NO.	RECEIVED FROM	ACCT. NO.	AMOUNT		DATE OF DEPOSIT	CHECK NO.	RECEIVED FROM	ACCT. NO.	AMOUNT	
			TOTAL FORWARD				**TOTAL INCOME THIS MONTH**				

MONTHLY SUMMARY
CASH BASIS

Month of _____

INCOME

ACCT. NO.	ACCOUNT	TOTAL THIS MONTH		TOTAL TO LAST MONTH		TOTAL TO DATE	
101	"F" Horse Sales						
102	"4797" Horse Sales						
103	Home-Grown Sales						
104	Sales						
105	Boarding						
106	Commission						
107	Leasing						
108	Lessons/Riding-Training						
109	Prize Money						
110	Stable Fees						
111	Other - Miscellaneous						
112	Other - Shoeing						
113	Other - Braiding						
114	Other - Personal						
115	Other - Grooming						
116	Other - Breeding Income						
117							
118							
119							
120							
121							
	Total This Month						
	Total To Last Month						
	Total To Date						

DISBURSEMENTS

ACCT. NO.	ACCOUNT	TOTAL THIS MONTH		TOTAL TO LAST MONTH		TOTAL TO DATE	
201	Breeding						
202	Conservation						
203	Feed Purchased						
204	Fertilizer and Lime						
205	Freight Trucking						
206	Gas, Fuel, Oil						
207	Insurance						
208	Land Clearing						
209	Labor Hired						
210	Machine Hire						
211	Mortgage Interest						
212	Other Interest						
213	Rent of Farm						
214	Repairs Maintenance						
215	Supplies Purchased						
216	Taxes						
217	Veterinary Fees						
218	Advertising						
219	Blacksmith						
220	Board						
221	Dues & Subscriptions						
222	Education						
223	Entertainment & Travel						
224	Entry Fees						
225	Legal & Accounting						
226	Office						
227	Personal						
228	Telephone						
229	Training/Transportation of Horse						
230	Other						
301	Horse for Investment or Use						
301	Horse for Resale						
	TOTAL THIS MONTH						
	TOTAL TO LAST MONTH						
	TOTAL TO DATE						

PROFIT AND (LOSS)

Total Income This Month _____

Less Total Disbursements This Month _____

Profit (Loss) This Month _____

Total Income To Date _____

Less Total Disbursements To Date _____

Profit (Loss) To Date _____

CASH DISBURSEMENTS
CASH BASIS

Month of _____

DATE	CHECK NO.	PAYEE	ITEM & QUANTITY	ACCT. NO.	AMOUNT	
				TOTAL FORWARD		

CASH DISBURSEMENTS *(continued)*

Month of _____

DATE	CHECK NO.	PAYEE	ITEM & QUANTITY	ACCT. NO.	AMOUNT	
			TOTAL FORWARDED			
				TOTAL CASH DISBURSEMENTS THIS MONTH			

INCOME
CASH BASIS

Month of _____

DATE OF DEPOSIT	CHECK NO.	RECEIVED FROM	ACCT. NO.	AMOUNT		DATE OF DEPOSIT	CHECK NO.	RECEIVED FROM	ACCT. NO.	AMOUNT	
			TOTAL FORWARD					***TOTAL INCOME THIS MONTH***			

MONTHLY SUMMARY
CASH BASIS

Month of _____

INCOME

ACCT. NO.	ACCOUNT	TOTAL THIS MONTH		TOTAL TO LAST MONTH		TOTAL TO DATE	
101	"F" Horse Sales						
102	"4797" Horse Sales						
103	Home-Grown Sales						
104	Sales						
105	Boarding						
106	Commission						
107	Leasing						
108	Lessons/Riding-Training						
109	Prize Money						
110	Stable Fees						
111	Other - Miscellaneous						
112	Other - Shoeing						
113	Other - Braiding						
114	Other - Personal						
115	Other - Grooming						
116	Other - Breeding Income						
117							
118							
119							
120							
121							
Total This Month							
Total To Last Month							
Total To Date							

DISBURSEMENTS

ACCT. NO.	ACCOUNT	TOTAL THIS MONTH		TOTAL TO LAST MONTH		TOTAL TO DATE	
201	Breeding						
202	Conservation						
203	Feed Purchased						
204	Fertilizer and Lime						
205	Freight Trucking						
206	Gas, Fuel, Oil						
207	Insurance						
208	Land Clearing						
209	Labor Hired						
210	Machine Hire						
211	Mortgage Interest						
212	Other Interest						
213	Rent of Farm						
214	Repairs Maintenance						
215	Supplies Purchased						
216	Taxes						
217	Veterinary Fees						
218	Advertising						
219	Blacksmith						
220	Board						
221	Dues & Subscriptions						
222	Education						
223	Entertainment & Travel						
224	Entry Fees						
225	Legal & Accounting						
226	Office						
227	Personal						
228	Telephone						
229	Training/Transportation of Horse						
230	Other						
301	Horse for Investment or Use						
301	Horse for Resale						
TOTAL THIS MONTH							
TOTAL TO LAST MONTH							
TOTAL TO DATE							

PROFIT AND (LOSS)

Total Income This Month _____

Less Total Disbursements This Month _____

Profit (Loss) This Month _____

Total Income To Date _____

Less Total Disbursements To Date _____

Profit (Loss) To Date _____

CASH DISBURSEMENTS

Month of _____   **CASH BASIS**

DATE	CHECK NO.	PAYEE	ITEM & QUANTITY	ACCT. NO.	AMOUNT	
				TOTAL FORWARD		

CASH DISBURSEMENTS *(continued)*

Month of _____

DATE	CHECK NO.	PAYEE	ITEM & QUANTITY	ACCT. NO.	AMOUNT	
			TOTAL FORWARDED			
			TOTAL CASH DISBURSEMENTS THIS MONTH			

INCOME
CASH BASIS

Month of _____

DATE OF DEPOSIT	CHECK NO.	RECEIVED FROM	ACCT. NO.	AMOUNT		DATE OF DEPOSIT	CHECK NO.	RECEIVED FROM	ACCT. NO.	AMOUNT	
						TOTAL INCOME THIS MONTH				
		TOTAL FORWARD									

MONTHLY SUMMARY
CASH BASIS

Month of _____

INCOME

ACCT. NO.	ACCOUNT	TOTAL THIS MONTH		TOTAL TO LAST MONTH		TOTAL TO DATE	
101	"F" Horse Sales						
102	"4797" Horse Sales						
103	Home-Grown Sales						
104	Sales						
105	Boarding						
106	Commission						
107	Leasing						
108	Lessons/Riding-Training						
109	Prize Money						
110	Stable Fees						
111	Other - Miscellaneous						
112	Other - Shoeing						
113	Other - Braiding						
114	Other - Personal						
115	Other - Grooming						
116	Other - Breeding Income						
117							
118							
119							
120							
121							
	Total This Month						
	Total To Last Month						
	Total To Date						

DISBURSEMENTS

ACCT. NO.	ACCOUNT	TOTAL THIS MONTH		TOTAL TO LAST MONTH		TOTAL TO DATE	
201	Breeding						
202	Conservation						
203	Feed Purchased						
204	Fertilizer and Lime						
205	Freight Trucking						
206	Gas, Fuel, Oil						
207	Insurance						
208	Land Clearing						
209	Labor Hired						
210	Machine Hire						
211	Mortgage Interest						
212	Other Interest						
213	Rent of Farm						
214	Repairs Maintenance						
215	Supplies Purchased						
216	Taxes						
217	Veterinary Fees						
218	Advertising						
219	Blacksmith						
220	Board						
221	Dues & Subscriptions						
222	Education						
223	Entertainment & Travel						
224	Entry Fees						
225	Legal & Accounting						
226	Office						
227	Personal						
228	Telephone						
229	Training/Transportation of Horse						
230	Other						
301	Horse for Investment or Use						
301	Horse for Resale						
	TOTAL THIS MONTH						
	TOTAL TO LAST MONTH						
	TOTAL TO DATE						

PROFIT AND (LOSS)

Total Income This Month _____

Less Total Disbursements This Month _____

Profit (Loss) This Month _____

Total Income To Date _____

Less Total Disbursements To Date _____

Profit (Loss) To Date _____

CASH DISBURSEMENTS

Month of _____   **CASH BASIS**

DATE	CHECK NO.	PAYEE	ITEM & QUANTITY	ACCT. NO.	AMOUNT	
				TOTAL FORWARD		

CASH DISBURSEMENTS *(continued)*

Month of _____

DATE	CHECK NO.	PAYEE	ITEM & QUANTITY	ACCT. NO.	AMOUNT	
			TOTAL FORWARDED			
			TOTAL CASH DISBURSEMENTS THIS MONTH			

INCOME
CASH BASIS

Month of _____

DATE OF DEPOSIT	CHECK NO.	RECEIVED FROM	ACCT. NO.	AMOUNT		DATE OF DEPOSIT	CHECK NO.	RECEIVED FROM	ACCT. NO.	AMOUNT	
				TOTAL FORWARD				*TOTAL INCOME THIS MONTH*			

MONTHLY SUMMARY
CASH BASIS

Month of _____

INCOME

ACCT. NO.	ACCOUNT	TOTAL THIS MONTH		TOTAL TO LAST MONTH		TOTAL TO DATE	
101	"F" Horse Sales						
102	"4797" Horse Sales						
103	Home-Grown Sales						
104	Sales						
105	Boarding						
106	Commission						
107	Leasing						
108	Lessons/Riding-Training						
109	Prize Money						
110	Stable Fees						
111	Other - Miscellaneous						
112	Other - Shoeing						
113	Other - Braiding						
114	Other - Personal						
115	Other - Grooming						
116	Other - Breeding Income						
117							
118							
119							
120							
121							
Total This Month							
Total To Last Month							
Total To Date							

PROFIT AND (LOSS)

Total Income This Month _____

Less Total Disbursements This Month _____

Profit (Loss) This Month _____

Total Income To Date _____

Less Total Disbursements To Date _____

Profit (Loss) To Date _____

DISBURSEMENTS

ACCT. NO.	ACCOUNT	TOTAL THIS MONTH		TOTAL TO LAST MONTH		TOTAL TO DATE	
201	Breeding						
202	Conservation						
203	Feed Purchased						
204	Fertilizer and Lime						
205	Freight Trucking						
206	Gas, Fuel, Oil						
207	Insurance						
208	Land Clearing						
209	Labor Hired						
210	Machine Hire						
211	Mortgage Interest						
212	Other Interest						
213	Rent of Farm						
214	Repairs Maintenance						
215	Supplies Purchased						
216	Taxes						
217	Veterinary Fees						
218	Advertising						
219	Blacksmith						
220	Board						
221	Dues & Subscriptions						
222	Education						
223	Entertainment & Travel						
224	Entry Fees						
225	Legal & Accounting						
226	Office						
227	Personal						
228	Telephone						
229	Training/Transportation of Horse						
230	Other						
301	Horse for Investment or Use						
301	Horse for Resale						
TOTAL THIS MONTH							
TOTAL TO LAST MONTH							
TOTAL TO DATE							

CASH DISBURSEMENTS

Month of _____

CASH BASIS

DATE	CHECK NO.	PAYEE	ITEM & QUANTITY	ACCT. NO.	AMOUNT	
				TOTAL FORWARD		

CASH DISBURSEMENTS *(continued)*

Month of _____

DATE	CHECK NO.	PAYEE	ITEM & QUANTITY	ACCT. NO.	AMOUNT
			TOTAL FORWARDED		
			TOTAL CASH DISBURSEMENTS THIS MONTH		

INCOME
CASH BASIS

Month of _____

DATE OF DEPOSIT	CHECK NO.	RECEIVED FROM	ACCT. NO.	AMOUNT		DATE OF DEPOSIT	CHECK NO.	RECEIVED FROM	ACCT. NO.	AMOUNT	
			TOTAL FORWARD					*TOTAL INCOME THIS MONTH*			

MONTHLY SUMMARY
CASH BASIS

Month of _____

INCOME

ACCT. NO.	ACCOUNT	TOTAL THIS MONTH		TOTAL TO LAST MONTH		TOTAL TO DATE	
101	"F" Horse Sales						
102	"4797" Horse Sales						
103	Home-Grown Sales						
104	Sales						
105	Boarding						
106	Commission						
107	Leasing						
108	Lessons/Riding-Training						
109	Prize Money						
110	Stable Fees						
111	Other - Miscellaneous						
112	Other - Shoeing						
113	Other - Braiding						
114	Other - Personal						
115	Other - Grooming						
116	Other - Breeding Income						
117							
118							
119							
120							
121							
	Total This Month						
	Total To Last Month						
	Total To Date						

PROFIT AND (LOSS)

Total Income This Month _____

Less Total Disbursements This Month _____

Profit (Loss) This Month _____

Total Income To Date _____

Less Total Disbursements To Date _____

Profit (Loss) To Date _____

DISBURSEMENTS

ACCT. NO.	ACCOUNT	TOTAL THIS MONTH		TOTAL TO LAST MONTH		TOTAL TO DATE	
201	Breeding						
202	Conservation						
203	Feed Purchased						
204	Fertilizer and Lime						
205	Freight Trucking						
206	Gas, Fuel, Oil						
207	Insurance						
208	Land Clearing						
209	Labor Hired						
210	Machine Hire						
211	Mortgage Interest						
212	Other Interest						
213	Rent of Farm						
214	Repairs Maintenance						
215	Supplies Purchased						
216	Taxes						
217	Veterinary Fees						
218	Advertising						
219	Blacksmith						
220	Board						
221	Dues & Subscriptions						
222	Education						
223	Entertainment & Travel						
224	Entry Fees						
225	Legal & Accounting						
226	Office						
227	Personal						
228	Telephone						
229	Training/Transportation of Horse						
230	Other						
301	Horse for Investment or Use						
301	Horse for Resale						
	TOTAL THIS MONTH						
	TOTAL TO LAST MONTH						
	TOTAL TO DATE						

CASH DISBURSEMENTS

CASH BASIS

Month of _____

DATE	CHECK NO.	PAYEE	ITEM & QUANTITY	ACCT. NO.	AMOUNT	
			TOTAL FORWARD			

CASH DISBURSEMENTS (continued)

Month of _____

DATE	CHECK NO.	PAYEE	ITEM & QUANTITY	ACCT. NO.	AMOUNT	
			TOTAL FORWARDED			
			TOTAL CASH DISBURSEMENTS THIS MONTH			

INCOME
CASH BASIS

Month of _____

DATE OF DEPOSIT	CHECK NO.	RECEIVED FROM	ACCT. NO.	AMOUNT		DATE OF DEPOSIT	CHECK NO.	RECEIVED FROM	ACCT. NO.	AMOUNT	
			TOTAL FORWARD					*TOTAL INCOME THIS MONTH*			

MONTHLY SUMMARY
CASH BASIS

Month of _____

INCOME

ACCT. NO.	ACCOUNT	TOTAL THIS MONTH		TOTAL TO LAST MONTH		TOTAL TO DATE	
101	"F" Horse Sales						
102	"4797" Horse Sales						
103	Home-Grown Sales						
104	Sales						
105	Boarding						
106	Commission						
107	Leasing						
108	Lessons/Riding-Training						
109	Prize Money						
110	Stable Fees						
111	Other - Miscellaneous						
112	Other - Shoeing						
113	Other - Braiding						
114	Other - Personal						
115	Other - Grooming						
116	Other - Breeding Income						
117							
118							
119							
120							
121							
Total This Month							
Total To Last Month							
Total To Date							

PROFIT AND (LOSS)

Total Income This Month _____

Less Total Disbursements This Month _____

Profit (Loss) This Month _____

Total Income To Date _____

Less Total Disbursements To Date _____

Profit (Loss) To Date _____

DISBURSEMENTS

ACCT. NO.	ACCOUNT	TOTAL THIS MONTH		TOTAL TO LAST MONTH		TOTAL TO DATE	
201	Breeding						
202	Conservation						
203	Feed Purchased						
204	Fertilizer and Lime						
205	Freight Trucking						
206	Gas, Fuel, Oil						
207	Insurance						
208	Land Clearing						
209	Labor Hired						
210	Machine Hire						
211	Mortgage Interest						
212	Other Interest						
213	Rent of Farm						
214	Repairs Maintenance						
215	Supplies Purchased						
216	Taxes						
217	Veterinary Fees						
218	Advertising						
219	Blacksmith						
220	Board						
221	Dues & Subscriptions						
222	Education						
223	Entertainment & Travel						
224	Entry Fees						
225	Legal & Accounting						
226	Office						
227	Personal						
228	Telephone						
229	Training/Transportation of Horse						
230	Other						
301	Horse for Investment or Use						
301	Horse for Resale						
TOTAL THIS MONTH							
TOTAL TO LAST MONTH							
TOTAL TO DATE							

CASH DISBURSEMENTS
CASH BASIS

Month of _____

DATE	CHECK NO.	PAYEE	ITEM & QUANTITY	ACCT. NO.	AMOUNT	
				TOTAL FORWARD		

CASH DISBURSEMENTS *(continued)*

Month of _____

DATE	CHECK NO.	PAYEE	ITEM & QUANTITY	ACCT. NO.	AMOUNT	
			TOTAL FORWARDED			
			TOTAL CASH DISBURSEMENTS THIS MONTH			

INCOME
CASH BASIS

Month of _____

DATE OF DEPOSIT	CHECK NO.	RECEIVED FROM	ACCT. NO.	AMOUNT		DATE OF DEPOSIT	CHECK NO.	RECEIVED FROM	ACCT. NO.	AMOUNT	
		TOTAL FORWARD						*TOTAL INCOME THIS MONTH*			

MONTHLY SUMMARY
CASH BASIS

Month of _____

INCOME

ACCT. NO.	ACCOUNT	TOTAL THIS MONTH	TOTAL TO LAST MONTH	TOTAL TO DATE
101	"F" Horse Sales			
102	"4797" Horse Sales			
103	Home-Grown Sales			
104	Sales			
105	Boarding			
106	Commission			
107	Leasing			
108	Lessons/Riding-Training			
109	Prize Money			
110	Stable Fees			
111	Other - Miscellaneous			
112	Other - Shoeing			
113	Other - Braiding			
114	Other - Personal			
115	Other - Grooming			
116	Other - Breeding Income			
117				
118				
119				
120				
121				
	Total This Month			
	Total To Last Month			
	Total To Date			

DISBURSEMENTS

ACCT. NO.	ACCOUNT	TOTAL THIS MONTH	TOTAL TO LAST MONTH	TOTAL TO DATE
201	Breeding			
202	Conservation			
203	Feed Purchased			
204	Fertilizer and Lime			
205	Freight Trucking			
206	Gas, Fuel, Oil			
207	Insurance			
208	Land Clearing			
209	Labor Hired			
210	Machine Hire			
211	Mortgage Interest			
212	Other Interest			
213	Rent of Farm			
214	Repairs Maintenance			
215	Supplies Purchased			
216	Taxes			
217	Veterinary Fees			
218	Advertising			
219	Blacksmith			
220	Board			
221	Dues & Subscriptions			
222	Education			
223	Entertainment & Travel			
224	Entry Fees			
225	Legal & Accounting			
226	Office			
227	Personal			
228	Telephone			
229	Training/Transportation of Horse			
230	Other			
301	Horse for Investment or Use			
301	Horse for Resale			
	TOTAL THIS MONTH			
	TOTAL TO LAST MONTH			
	TOTAL TO DATE			

PROFIT AND (LOSS)

Total Income This Month _____

Less Total Disbursements This Month _____

Profit (Loss) This Month _____

Total Income To Date _____

Less Total Disbursements To Date _____

Profit (Loss) To Date _____

CLIENT ACCOUNT RECORD
ACCRUAL OR CASH BASIS

Name of Client:

Address:

Telephone:

DATE	DEBIT		CREDIT		BALANCE		DATE	DEBIT		CREDIT		BALANCE	

SALES JOURNAL
ACCRUAL BASIS

Month of _____

A ACCOUNTS RECEIVABLE		INCOME			E SALES TAX		F MISCELLANEOUS	
		B BOARD	C TRAINING	D HORSE SALES				

CASH RECEIPTS
ACCRUAL BASIS

Month of _____

A DEPOSIT AMOUNT		B ACCT. RECEIVABLE		C OTHER ITEM	AMOUNT		A DEPOSIT AMOUNT		B ACCT. RECEIVABLE		C OTHER ITEM	AMOUNT	

ACCOUNTS PAYABLE
ACCRUAL BASIS

Month of _____

VENDOR	A ACCOUNTS PAYABLE		ITEM	B EXPENSE AMOUNT		C OTHER AMOUNT	

ACCOUNTS PAYABLE
ACCRUAL BASIS

Month of _____

DATE	CHECK NO.	PAYEE	NET CHECK	PAYROLL WITHHOLDING				GROSS WAGE	ACCOUNT PAYABLE	EXPENSE ITEM	OTHER ITEM
				FICA	FEDERAL	STATE	DISABILITY				

DEPRECIATION SCHEDULE
ACCRUAL OR CASH BASIS

Year _____

A DESCRIPTION OF PROPERTY	B DATE PLACED IN SERVICE	C COST OR OTHER BASIS	D DEPRECIATION ALLOWED OR ALLOWABLE/YEAR	E METHOD	F LIFE OR RATE	G DEDUCTION THIS YEAR

ACTIVE PARTICIPATION JOURNAL

DATE	BRIEF DESCRIPTION OF ACTIVITY	TIME*
	* Based on .1=6 minutes; 1.0=1 hour **TOTAL:**	

INDIVIDUAL PAYROLL RECORD

YEAR _____

NAME   SOC. SEC. NO.

ADDRESS

NO. OF EXEMPTIONS   RATE OF PAY

	PAY DATE	CHECK NO.	PERIOD ENDING	SALARY	OVERTIME	GROSS WAGES	FEDERAL TAX	STATE TAX	FICA	DISABILITY INS.	MED. INS.	NET PAY
1												
2												
3												
4												
5												
6												
7												
8												
9												
10												
11												
12												
13												
TOTAL 1ST QUARTER												
YEAR TO DATE												
14												
15												
16												
17												
18												
19												
20												
21												
22												
23												
24												
25												
26												
TOTAL 2ND QUARTER												
YEAR TO DATE												
27												
28												
29												
30												
31												
32												
33												
34												
35												
36												
37												
38												
39												
TOTAL 3RD QUARTER												
YEAR TO DATE												
40												
41												
42												
43												
44												
45												
46												
47												
48												
49												
50												
51												
52												
TOTAL 4TH QUARTER												
TOTAL YEAR												

INDIVIDUAL PAYROLL RECORD

YEAR _____

NAME   SOC. SEC. NO.

ADDRESS

NO. OF EXEMPTIONS   RATE OF PAY

	PAY DATE	CHECK NO.	PERIOD ENDING	SALARY	OVERTIME	GROSS WAGES	FEDERAL TAX	STATE TAX	FICA	DISABILITY INS.	MED. INS.	NET PAY
1												
2												
3												
4												
5												
6												
7												
8												
9												
10												
11												
12												
13												
TOTAL 1ST QUARTER												
YEAR TO DATE												
14												
15												
16												
17												
18												
19												
20												
21												
22												
23												
24												
25												
26												
TOTAL 2ND QUARTER												
YEAR TO DATE												
27												
28												
29												
30												
31												
32												
33												
34												
35												
36												
37												
38												
39												
TOTAL 3RD QUARTER												
YEAR TO DATE												
40												
41												
42												
43												
44												
45												
46												
47												
48												
49												
50												
51												
52												
TOTAL 4TH QUARTER												
TOTAL YEAR												

DEDUCTIONS

INDIVIDUAL PAYROLL RECORD

YEAR _____

NAME _____ SOC. SEC. NO. _____

ADDRESS _____

NO. OF EXEMPTIONS _____ RATE OF PAY _____

	PAY DATE	CHECK NO.	PERIOD ENDING	SALARY	OVERTIME	GROSS WAGES	DEDUCTIONS					NET PAY
							FEDERAL TAX	STATE TAX	FICA	DISABILITY INS.	MED. INS.	
1												
2												
3												
4												
5												
6												
7												
8												
9												
10												
11												
12												
13												
TOTAL 1ST QUARTER												
YEAR TO DATE												
14												
15												
16												
17												
18												
19												
20												
21												
22												
23												
24												
25												
26												
TOTAL 2ND QUARTER												
YEAR TO DATE												
27												
28												
29												
30												
31												
32												
33												
34												
35												
36												
37												
38												
39												
TOTAL 3RD QUARTER												
YEAR TO DATE												
40												
41												
42												
43												
44												
45												
46												
47												
48												
49												
50												
51												
52												
TOTAL 4TH QUARTER												
TOTAL YEAR												

INDIVIDUAL PAYROLL RECORD

YEAR _____

NAME _____ SOC. SEC. NO. _____

ADDRESS

NO. OF EXEMPTIONS   RATE OF PAY

| | PAY DATE | CHECK NO. | PERIOD ENDING | SALARY | OVERTIME | GROSS WAGES | DEDUCTIONS | | | | | NET PAY |
							FEDERAL TAX	STATE TAX	FICA	DISABILITY INS.	MED. INS.	
1												
2												
3												
4												
5												
6												
7												
8												
9												
10												
11												
12												
13												
TOTAL 1ST QUARTER												
YEAR TO DATE												
14												
15												
16												
17												
18												
19												
20												
21												
22												
23												
24												
25												
26												
TOTAL 2ND QUARTER												
YEAR TO DATE												
27												
28												
29												
30												
31												
32												
33												
34												
35												
36												
37												
38												
39												
TOTAL 3RD QUARTER												
YEAR TO DATE												
40												
41												
42												
43												
44												
45												
46												
47												
48												
49												
50												
51												
52												
TOTAL 4TH QUARTER												
TOTAL YEAR												

INDIVIDUAL PAYROLL RECORD

YEAR _____

NAME _____ SOC. SEC. NO. _____

ADDRESS _____

NO. OF EXEMPTIONS _____ RATE OF PAY _____

	PAY DATE	CHECK NO.	PERIOD ENDING	SALARY	OVERTIME	GROSS WAGES	FEDERAL TAX	STATE TAX	FICA	DISABILITY INS.	MED. INS.	NET PAY
							DEDUCTIONS					
1												
2												
3												
4												
5												
6												
7												
8												
9												
10												
11												
12												
13												
TOTAL 1ST QUARTER												
YEAR TO DATE												
14												
15												
16												
17												
18												
19												
20												
21												
22												
23												
24												
25												
26												
TOTAL 2ND QUARTER												
YEAR TO DATE												
27												
28												
29												
30												
31												
32												
33												
34												
35												
36												
37												
38												
39												
TOTAL 3RD QUARTER												
YEAR TO DATE												
40												
41												
42												
43												
44												
45												
46												
47												
48												
49												
50												
51												
52												
TOTAL 4TH QUARTER												
TOTAL YEAR												

INDIVIDUAL PAYROLL RECORD

YEAR _____

NAME   SOC. SEC. NO.

ADDRESS

NO. OF EXEMPTIONS   RATE OF PAY

	PAY DATE	CHECK NO.	PERIOD ENDING	SALARY		OVERTIME		GROSS WAGES	FEDERAL TAX	STATE TAX	FICA	DISABILITY INS.	MED. INS.	NET PAY	
									DEDUCTIONS						
1															
2															
3															
4															
5															
6															
7															
8															
9															
10															
11															
12															
13															
TOTAL 1ST QUARTER															
YEAR TO DATE															
14															
15															
16															
17															
18															
19															
20															
21															
22															
23															
24															
25															
26															
TOTAL 2ND QUARTER															
YEAR TO DATE															
27															
28															
29															
30															
31															
32															
33															
34															
35															
36															
37															
38															
39															
TOTAL 3RD QUARTER															
YEAR TO DATE															
40															
41															
42															
43															
44															
45															
46															
47															
48															
49															
50															
51															
52															
TOTAL 4TH QUARTER															
TOTAL YEAR															

INDIVIDUAL PAYROLL RECORD

YEAR _____

NAME _____ SOC. SEC. NO. _____

ADDRESS _____

NO. OF EXEMPTIONS _____ RATE OF PAY _____

	PAY DATE	CHECK NO.	PERIOD ENDING	SALARY	OVERTIME	GROSS WAGES	DEDUCTIONS					NET PAY
							FEDERAL TAX	STATE TAX	FICA	DISABILITY INS.	MED. INS.	
1												
2												
3												
4												
5												
6												
7												
8												
9												
10												
11												
12												
13												
TOTAL 1ST QUARTER												
YEAR TO DATE												
14												
15												
16												
17												
18												
19												
20												
21												
22												
23												
24												
25												
26												
TOTAL 2ND QUARTER												
YEAR TO DATE												
27												
28												
29												
30												
31												
32												
33												
34												
35												
36												
37												
38												
39												
TOTAL 3RD QUARTER												
YEAR TO DATE												
40												
41												
42												
43												
44												
45												
46												
47												
48												
49												
50												
51												
52												
TOTAL 4TH QUARTER												
TOTAL YEAR												

INDIVIDUAL PAYROLL RECORD

YEAR _____

NAME _____ SOC. SEC. NO. _____

ADDRESS

NO. OF EXEMPTIONS _____ RATE OF PAY _____

	PAY DATE	CHECK NO.	PERIOD ENDING	SALARY	OVERTIME	GROSS WAGES	DEDUCTIONS					NET PAY
							FEDERAL TAX	STATE TAX	FICA	DISABILITY INS.	MED. INS.	
1												
2												
3												
4												
5												
6												
7												
8												
9												
10												
11												
12												
13												
TOTAL 1ST QUARTER												
YEAR TO DATE												
14												
15												
16												
17												
18												
19												
20												
21												
22												
23												
24												
25												
26												
TOTAL 2ND QUARTER												
YEAR TO DATE												
27												
28												
29												
30												
31												
32												
33												
34												
35												
36												
37												
38												
39												
TOTAL 3RD QUARTER												
YEAR TO DATE												
40												
41												
42												
43												
44												
45												
46												
47												
48												
49												
50												
51												
52												
TOTAL 4TH QUARTER												
TOTAL YEAR												

INDIVIDUAL PAYROLL RECORD

YEAR _____

NAME _____ SOC. SEC. NO. _____

ADDRESS _____

NO. OF EXEMPTIONS _____ RATE OF PAY _____

	PAY DATE	CHECK NO.	PERIOD ENDING	SALARY	OVERTIME	GROSS WAGES	DEDUCTIONS					NET PAY
							FEDERAL TAX	STATE TAX	FICA	DISABILITY INS.	MED. INS.	
1												
2												
3												
4												
5												
6												
7												
8												
9												
10												
11												
12												
13												
TOTAL 1ST QUARTER												
YEAR TO DATE												
14												
15												
16												
17												
18												
19												
20												
21												
22												
23												
24												
25												
26												
TOTAL 2ND QUARTER												
YEAR TO DATE												
27												
28												
29												
30												
31												
32												
33												
34												
35												
36												
37												
38												
39												
TOTAL 3RD QUARTER												
YEAR TO DATE												
40												
41												
42												
43												
44												
45												
46												
47												
48												
49												
50												
51												
52												
TOTAL 4TH QUARTER												
TOTAL YEAR												

INDIVIDUAL PAYROLL RECORD

YEAR _____

NAME _____ SOC. SEC. NO. _____

ADDRESS _____

NO. OF EXEMPTIONS _____ RATE OF PAY _____

	PAY DATE	CHECK NO.	PERIOD ENDING	SALARY	OVERTIME	GROSS WAGES	FEDERAL TAX	STATE TAX	FICA	DISABILITY INS.	MED. INS.	NET PAY
							DEDUCTIONS					
1												
2												
3												
4												
5												
6												
7												
8												
9												
10												
11												
12												
13												
TOTAL 1ST QUARTER												
YEAR TO DATE												
14												
15												
16												
17												
18												
19												
20												
21												
22												
23												
24												
25												
26												
TOTAL 2ND QUARTER												
YEAR TO DATE												
27												
28												
29												
30												
31												
32												
33												
34												
35												
36												
37												
38												
39												
TOTAL 3RD QUARTER												
YEAR TO DATE												
40												
41												
42												
43												
44												
45												
46												
47												
48												
49												
50												
51												
52												
TOTAL 4TH QUARTER												
TOTAL YEAR												

INDIVIDUAL PAYROLL RECORD

YEAR _____

NAME _____ SOC. SEC. NO. _____

ADDRESS _____

NO. OF EXEMPTIONS _____ RATE OF PAY _____

	PAY DATE	CHECK NO.	PERIOD ENDING	SALARY		OVERTIME		GROSS WAGES	FEDERAL TAX	STATE TAX		FICA		DISABILITY INS.		MED. INS.		NET PAY	
									DEDUCTIONS											
1																				
2																				
3																				
4																				
5																				
6																				
7																				
8																				
9																				
10																				
11																				
12																				
13																				
TOTAL 1ST QUARTER																				
YEAR TO DATE																				
14																				
15																				
16																				
17																				
18																				
19																				
20																				
21																				
22																				
23																				
24																				
25																				
26																				
TOTAL 2ND QUARTER																				
YEAR TO DATE																				
27																				
28																				
29																				
30																				
31																				
32																				
33																				
34																				
35																				
36																				
37																				
38																				
39																				
TOTAL 3RD QUARTER																				
YEAR TO DATE																				
40																				
41																				
42																				
43																				
44																				
45																				
46																				
47																				
48																				
49																				
50																				
51																				
52																				
TOTAL 4TH QUARTER																				
TOTAL YEAR																				

INDIVIDUAL PAYROLL RECORD

YEAR _____

NAME _____ SOC. SEC. NO. _____

ADDRESS _____

NO. OF EXEMPTIONS _____ RATE OF PAY _____

	PAY DATE	CHECK NO.	PERIOD ENDING	SALARY	OVERTIME	GROSS WAGES	FEDERAL TAX	STATE TAX	FICA	DISABILITY INS.	MED. INS.	NET PAY
									DEDUCTIONS			
1												
2												
3												
4												
5												
6												
7												
8												
9												
10												
11												
12												
13												
TOTAL 1ST QUARTER												
YEAR TO DATE												
14												
15												
16												
17												
18												
19												
20												
21												
22												
23												
24												
25												
26												
TOTAL 2ND QUARTER												
YEAR TO DATE												
27												
28												
29												
30												
31												
32												
33												
34												
35												
36												
37												
38												
39												
TOTAL 3RD QUARTER												
YEAR TO DATE												
40												
41												
42												
43												
44												
45												
46												
47												
48												
49												
50												
51												
52												
TOTAL 4TH QUARTER												
TOTAL YEAR												

INDIVIDUAL PAYROLL RECORD

YEAR _____

NAME _____ SOC. SEC. NO. _____

ADDRESS _____

NO. OF EXEMPTIONS _____ RATE OF PAY _____

| | PAY DATE | CHECK NO. | PERIOD ENDING | SALARY | OVERTIME | GROSS WAGES | DEDUCTIONS | | | | | NET PAY |
							FEDERAL TAX	STATE TAX	FICA	DISABILITY INS.	MED. INS.	
1												
2												
3												
4												
5												
6												
7												
8												
9												
10												
11												
12												
13												
TOTAL 1ST QUARTER												
YEAR TO DATE												
14												
15												
16												
17												
18												
19												
20												
21												
22												
23												
24												
25												
26												
TOTAL 2ND QUARTER												
YEAR TO DATE												
27												
28												
29												
30												
31												
32												
33												
34												
35												
36												
37												
38												
39												
TOTAL 3RD QUARTER												
YEAR TO DATE												
40												
41												
42												
43												
44												
45												
46												
47												
48												
49												
50												
51												
52												
TOTAL 4TH QUARTER												
TOTAL YEAR												

INDIVIDUAL PAYROLL RECORD

YEAR _____

NAME _____ SOC. SEC. NO. _____

ADDRESS _____

NO. OF EXEMPTIONS _____ RATE OF PAY _____

	PAY DATE	CHECK NO.	PERIOD ENDING	SALARY	OVERTIME	GROSS WAGES	FEDERAL TAX	STATE TAX	FICA	DISABILITY INS.	MED. INS.	NET PAY
							DEDUCTIONS					
1												
2												
3												
4												
5												
6												
7												
8												
9												
10												
11												
12												
13												
TOTAL 1ST QUARTER												
YEAR TO DATE												
14												
15												
16												
17												
18												
19												
20												
21												
22												
23												
24												
25												
26												
TOTAL 2ND QUARTER												
YEAR TO DATE												
27												
28												
29												
30												
31												
32												
33												
34												
35												
36												
37												
38												
39												
TOTAL 3RD QUARTER												
YEAR TO DATE												
40												
41												
42												
43												
44												
45												
46												
47												
48												
49												
50												
51												
52												
TOTAL 4TH QUARTER												
TOTAL YEAR												

INDIVIDUAL PAYROLL RECORD

YEAR _____

NAME _____ SOC. SEC. NO. _____

ADDRESS _____

NO. OF EXEMPTIONS _____ RATE OF PAY _____

	PAY DATE	CHECK NO.	PERIOD ENDING	SALARY	OVERTIME	GROSS WAGES	DEDUCTIONS					NET PAY
							FEDERAL TAX	STATE TAX	FICA	DISABILITY INS.	MED. INS.	
1												
2												
3												
4												
5												
6												
7												
8												
9												
10												
11												
12												
13												
TOTAL 1ST QUARTER												
YEAR TO DATE												
14												
15												
16												
17												
18												
19												
20												
21												
22												
23												
24												
25												
26												
TOTAL 2ND QUARTER												
YEAR TO DATE												
27												
28												
29												
30												
31												
32												
33												
34												
35												
36												
37												
38												
39												
TOTAL 3RD QUARTER												
YEAR TO DATE												
40												
41												
42												
43												
44												
45												
46												
47												
48												
49												
50												
51												
52												
TOTAL 4TH QUARTER												
TOTAL YEAR												

INDIVIDUAL PAYROLL RECORD

YEAR _____

NAME _____ SOC. SEC. NO. _____

ADDRESS _____

NO. OF EXEMPTIONS _____ RATE OF PAY _____

	PAY DATE	CHECK NO.	PERIOD ENDING	SALARY	OVERTIME	GROSS WAGES	FEDERAL TAX	STATE TAX	FICA	DISABILITY INS.	MED. INS.	NET PAY
								DEDUCTIONS				
1												
2												
3												
4												
5												
6												
7												
8												
9												
10												
11												
12												
13												
TOTAL 1ST QUARTER												
YEAR TO DATE												
14												
15												
16												
17												
18												
19												
20												
21												
22												
23												
24												
25												
26												
TOTAL 2ND QUARTER												
YEAR TO DATE												
27												
28												
29												
30												
31												
32												
33												
34												
35												
36												
37												
38												
39												
TOTAL 3RD QUARTER												
YEAR TO DATE												
40												
41												
42												
43												
44												
45												
46												
47												
48												
49												
50												
51												
52												
TOTAL 4TH QUARTER												
TOTAL YEAR												

MASTER PAYROLL RECORD

YEAR _____

WEEK OR PERIOD ENDING	GROSS WAGES ALL EMPLOYEES		DEDUCTIONS FEDERAL		STATE		FICA		DISAB.		MED. INS.		NET PAY		NOTES
1															
2															
3															
4															
5															
6															
7															
8															
9															
10															
11															
12															
13															
TOTAL 1ST QUARTER YEAR TO DATE															
14															
15															
16															
17															
18															
19															
20															
21															
22															
23															
24															
25															
26															
TOTAL 2ND QUARTER YEAR TO DATE															
27															
28															
29															
30															
31															
32															
33															
34															
35															
36															
37															
38															
39															
TOTAL 3RD QUARTER YEAR TO DATE															
40															
41															
42															
43															
44															
45															
46															
47															
48															
49															
50															
51															
52															
TOTAL 4TH QUARTER															
TOTAL YEAR															